MISS MINNIE BANNISTER
(Spinster of the Parish)

Although she refused to be quoted directly, some Sanders-style flattery induced Miss Bannister to reveal that she had once danced the Can-Can at the Windmill Theatre, and that in the naughty nineties she had been 'the darling of Roper's Light Horse'. She also hinted at a former passionate involvement with a bounder named Bloodnok. When pressed, however, she screamed and referred all further questions to her spokesman and companion of honour, Mr Henry Crun.

MR HENRY CRUN
(A thin ancient and inventor)

'Mnk – grnk – mnk – mnk – grmp.'
(Persistent questioning failed to refresh Mr. Crun's memory as to the identity of Mr Henry Crun, beyond the remark, 'Henry Crun? Mnk – isn't that the name of – mnk – Henry Crun?')

WILLIUM 'MATE' COBBLERS
(Drains cleared while you wait)

Born Shoreditch 1900, son of Fred "Chopper" Cobblers, OBE, road sweeper, and Vera Collins. Left school at 14. Joined Thomas Crapper & Son as tea boy. Joined Chislehurst Laundry as tea boy. Joined Woolwich Arsenal as tea boy. Conscripted for World War I as Private in Sappers and Miners as tea boy. Rose to rank of acting unpaid Lance Corporal – injured in action by tea urn falling on head. Mentioned in dispatches as "always moaning". Discharged in 1918, since when he has wandered the streets of London telling motorists, with no authority whatsoever, "You can't park there" or "Put that cigarette out" or "I don't know, I'm a stranger round here" or "Why don't you get yer 'air cut?" or "Two years in the army would do 'em good" or "Bloody foreigners" or "I spent 4 years fighting for this country." Now uniformed doorman at BBC Aeolian Hall, wears full war medals at all times, and King's badge for the disabled. Informs all visitors to the BBC, "It's nothing to do with me mate." Clubs: Bristol Legion. Recreations: saying "You can't park there", etc.

MAJOR DENIS BLOODNOK, IND. ARM. RTD.
(Military idiot, coward and bar)

Born 1867 and 1880, Sandhurst NAAFI. Served in S. African war – taken prisoner on first day under strange circumstances. Released by Boers after 3 days as being "unreliable". Spent the rest of the war in the Pay Corps. Large sums of money were in his keeping. They were never traced. Transferred to Aldershot Southern Command as Quartermaster General – was responsible for 30,000 rupees worth of stores. They were never traced. Military Police traced *him* to Rangoon, where he was found wearing false testicles in a Freak Show. Cashiered. Married the Hon. Mrs. Scrack-Thing. Divorced. Rejoined Army under an assumed height as Florence Bloodnok: served 1 year in ATS. His disguise became known when he reported a sailor for molesting him in an air-raid shelter. Using his position as a mason, he re-joined the Army as a Major; he saw action and suffered wounds in the bedroom of Mrs. Madge Feel. World War II – he was found hiding in a hut near Quetta, where he swore a solemn oath that he was an eccentric Hindu fakir who had gone white with fear. Cashiered for the 7th time – a world military record. Wearing a stocking mask, he rejoined the British Army as a Chinaman. Using masonic connections he became a Major again. Clubs: Anyone. Recreations: Piccadilly Circus. Hobbies: The Indian Army. Agent: Miss M. Bannister.

THE GOON SHOW SCRIPTS

First published in Great Britain in 1973 by
THE WOBURN PRESS
67 Great Russell Street,
London WC1B 3BT

ISBN 0 7130 0088 0

The publishers acknowledge with thanks
the co-operation of the BBC.

Acknowledgements are also due to: Radio Times for
permission to use their article by Ray Connolly and
photographs by Tony Evans; BBC Publicity Photograph
Library for photographs from the Michael Parkinson Show
Dave Silverman for his generous help with the
supply of tapes; The Goon Show Preservation Society
for their assistance with the Goonology.

Co-ordinating editor: Colin Webb
Designed by Harold King
Printed in Great Britain by C. J. Mason & Sons Ltd., Bristol
and bound by Robert Hartnoll Ltd., Bodmin, Cornwall

MORE
GOON SHOW
Scripts

Written and Selected by

SPIKE MILLIGAN

With drawings by

Peter Sellers

Harry Secombe

Spike Milligan

WOBURN PRESS

PUBLISHERS NOTE

In this second collection of Goon Show scripts, Spike Milligan has made his selection from the shows broadcast between December 1958 and February 1959. He has included shows that have since become legendary. 'Ned's Atomic Dustbin', for example, could almost qualify for the 'By Royal Appointment' tag. The publication of our first collection of scripts, together with the BBC's 'Last Goon Show of All', unleashed an overwhelming demand for material connected with the Goons and the shows. This demand is perhaps epitomised by the current success of the 'Ying Tong Song', which was recorded seventeen years ago. Archive material in the form of tapes, records, photographs etc., is still scarce, and consequently the scripts published in book form will become lasting documents of comedy in this genre, as well as providing the opportunity to celebrate formally the comic genius of the Goons. In this book we have incorporated a complete list of the titled shows, together with the dates of the original broadcasts, which will help the aficionado to keep track of material as it becomes available. We have received help with this from The Goon Show Preservation Society, who can be contacted at 7 Frances Gardens, Ramsgate, Kent. The aim of this society is to keep alive active interest in the Goon Shows.

We are, once again, grateful to the Goons for their help in preparing this book, and for allowing us to use the doodles and drawings that they improvised on the backs of scripts etc., during rehearsals, and to Norma Farnes for her patience and assistance with new material.

As with our previous volume, the scripts are reproduced here in their complete form. Where a performer's name is indicated, instead of a character's, the performer was either using his own voice, or the intonation will be indicated in brackets. Old sterling references have been retained in order to avoid devaluation. Instructions for tapes (GRAMS), and sound effects (F.X.) have been retained throughout. The importance of the latter to the success of the shows cannot be over emphasized, and it is perhaps pertinent to finish this note with Harry Secombe's anecdote from the 'Michael Parkinson Show': 'I remember Spike once wanted the effect of something being hit with a sockful of custard, and he got the lady at the canteen of the Camden Theatre to make him a custard, and she thought he had a bad stomach. She went and lovingly prepared this custard for him. She said "Here you are Spike, here's your custard", and he said "Thank you", and took his sock off and poured it in. He went downstairs and swung this sock round his head, hit it against the wall, but it didn't have the effect he wanted. So, a sockful of custard and no effect.'

CONTENTS

BUCKINGHAM PALACE

It has always been one of my profound regrets that I was not born ten years earlier than 1948, since I would then have had the pure, unbounded joy of listening avidly to the "Goons" each week. Instead, I only discovered that the Goon-type humour appealed to me with an hysterical totality just as the shows were drawing to a close. Then I discovered the Ying Tong Song in record form and almost at once I knew it by heart - the only song I do know by heart. I plagued everybody with its dulcet tones and "Solo for Raspberry Blower" to such an extent that when my small brothers heard a recording of the Goons for the first time they thought it was their elder brother!

I was delighted to hear that a second series of Goon scripts was to be published. I received something like six copies of the first edition from countless sources and I daresay I shall receive as many of the second, thereby ensuring an immense profit for someone! These new scripts will bring enormous pleasure to countless Goon fans whose devotion demonstrates the eternal quality of Goon humour. No matter how much "fashion" in humour changes, there will always be thousands of people whose minds are attuned to the kind of mental slapstick and imaginary cartoonery that typifies Goonery. For that reason I am always hoping that many more Goon shows in record form will be made available to their dotty and devoted supporters.

If you open this book upside down, you will bump into a thing called "Backword". This is a witty joke by a leek-eating Welshman called Secombe who has committed the unforgivable sin of "lesé Majesté". This is not a reference to an indolent Gallic Monarch, but stems from his cry of "Eccles for King!" "There's many a true word spoken in jest", they say! So beware, Milligan, Sellers, Secombe and Co......

Charles.

MILLIGAN'S WHO'S WHO~ PART 95

Eccles Homo Sapiens, also Ecco Homo. Part-time human being, height varies between 2 foot 6 inches, and 18 foot 3 inches, depending upon food, environment and bed size. At birth he was round and full of currants, and was baptised Eccles Cake. Schooling,—Mr Crollicks Establishment for the chronic fit. Spent 18 years in kindergarten. Adopted by Rich Sponsor,—private tutor of two years. Tutor committed to an Asylum. Rich Sponsor charged with trying to drown the boy child Eccles, also charged with throwing him off the Eiffel Tower (Eccles survived the fall) charged with laying Eccles in face of oncoming steam roller. Rich Sponsor honoured on Queen's Birthday. Destruction of Eccles medal first clasp. Eccles was next seen by the Captain of the H.M.S. Poisiden he was 120 miles South South East of the Lizard and eating a sandwich, when hailed by the H.M.S. Poisiden he replied 'I had one two, but the wheels came off'. Since then the Admiralty have charted his course. Currently reported to be sleeping peacefully on a rocky Atoll in the French Atomic Bombing Range.

Bloodnok, Denis Leonard b. 1893—Educated Repton, Eton, Oxford (Mrs Sims Tea Rooms). Commissioned Sandhurst 1913 attached Ropers Light Horse, Indian Army 1914. Reported killed in action two days before the outbreak of war. Found wandering in room 361 of Dorchester Hotel when questioned by police he replied 'I am Mrs Dorothy Crollics and I am innocent'. A medical examination followed which he enjoyed, saying to the gynaecologist 'I don't know who you are Sir, but you've done me such a power of good.' He was given a suit of clothes and a pound. Reappeared as a Colonel in the Rajputana Rifles, who he hit with a stick. In 1916 with the Germans advancing on Paris, he in Poona, ordered his Regiment to retreat 600 miles to the Madras Cricket Club. Bloodnok leading them from 1st class compartment on the railway. Arrested on arrival for travelling without a ticket he replied 'I am Mrs Dorothy Crollics. I am innocent'. He escaped from Yeroda Jail disguised as Ghandi, meantime the *real* Ghandi was arrested as Major Bloodnok. Meantime Bloodnok had contracted Chinese Dysentry, 3 buckets of it. A Parsee doctor had treated him with heated enemas. At the time of going to press Bloodnok's whereabouts is not known, although at Paddington Station heavy snoring has been coming from the left luggage locker 32.

INTERVIEW

This interview with the Goons, by Ray Connolly, appeared in the Radio Times on 28th September 1972. The photographs are by Tony Evans.

ROMMEL and his men were somewhere over the hill and across the desert, and for months Harry Secombe and the regiment he was in had been on his trail. A new batch of troops was called forward, a regiment with a dirty great big cannon, which was dug in at the top of an embankment. That night Harry Secombe and his comrades slept at the foot of the hill, safe behind the gun.

'All at once there was a terrible noise,' says Harry Secombe. 'The gun can't have been dug in properly – it jumped straight up into the air and came careering down the 150ft hill towards our tents.

'While we were recovering from the shock, a pale looking youth with a hurricane lamp came hurrying down the hill towards our tents saying: "Anybody seen our gun? Can we have our cannon back?" That was when I met Spike.

'Somehow we found that we had the same sense of humour. After I was demobbed I used to go round to Jimmy Grafton's pub, and it was there that I met Peter Sellers. I couldn't fail to be impressed by Peter, because I've never known anyone who is as good at impressions as he is. I was at the Windmill at the time with Michael Bentine and I remember saying how they just had to meet Spike. So then all four of us would go round and Jimmy Grafton, who's now my agent, would stand us free drinks while we'd mess around with a tape recorder. Eventually we began to attract attention and a producer called Pat Dixon gave *The Goon Show* its first chance.'

That was in 1951, and the show was successful immediately. Milligan, the writer, was the main architect, but he's quick to point out that the programme wouldn't have worked without the others.

'We all helped to create the characters. They just happened. There was no family planning for the Goons. The list of characters grew just like a family. If we wanted a schoolboy then Peter would do a schoolboy voice and that would be that. There were hundreds of different characters over the eight years that the show ran.'

Both Peter Sellers and Harry Secombe remembered the show with a greater degree of fondness than Spike Milligan appeared to when I interviewed each of them for this article.

'We used to look forward immensely to those Sunday meetings,' said Sellers. 'Every Sunday was a reunion, when we could meet at the Camden Theatre to record the shows. *The Goon Show* would then set us up for another week.'

'Yes,' said Secombe, 'we'd come alive on Sundays. It was like being let out of school. We'd be hysterical reading the scripts. Really some of the shows were incoherent. It was a great time for catch phrases and we'd suddenly find that people were taking them up and using them.'

Which did Milligan consider his favourite scripts? 'I can't remember any really,' said Spike – 'But what I also remember were the rows and fights between us and the part-time Hitlers who said "you can't park here" and "put out that cigarette." People who didn't care about the show.'

Harry Secombe remembers similar incidents with greater relish: 'One time at the Camden Theatre one of these blokes came across to Peter and told him to put his cigarette out and Peter ignored him. The next minute the bloke was back with his fireman's axe and belt on, and all his gear, saying "now will you put it out?"'

None of them ever delved into the humour of the Goons, although at one time it became intellectually fashionable to try to analyse its success. 'We used to get letters from dons and surgeons and judges and cab drivers,' says Sellers. 'And there would be articles dissecting the show.

'But some of the planners at the BBC didn't know what we were all about. I remember there was a story about a meeting of planners at Broadcasting House where the chairman is supposed to have said: "The first item is *The Go On Show*." And someone said: "No sir, Goon, sir." And he said: "Goon. What's a Goon? D'you mean *The Coon Show*...?"' The name Goon, says Secombe, came from a cartoon that

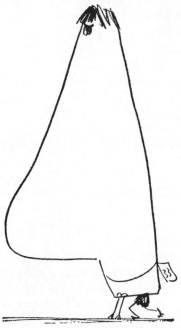

Spike Milligan by Sellers

was in the *Daily Mirror* before the war, where Popeye was stranded on a desert island with great hairy monsters who spoke in scribbles. 'And then the prisoners of war used to call the guards goons, so it came to mean any big idiot.'

The favourite character Eccles was, Spike Milligan admits, pinched from the cartoon character Goofy, for whom he had developed a fondness as a boy. Spike played Eccles, Moriarty and Minnie Bannister; Peter Sellers was

Bloodnock, Henry Crun, Bluebottle, Grytpype-Thynne and various other voices; while Harry Secombe was Neddy Seagoon.

'Once when Spike was ill, Peter played his parts too, and no one seemed to notice,' said Secombe. 'Of course Spike continued to write the scripts. He wrote some brilliant ones for us then. He had all the sweat of writing it, but for Peter and me it was just a giggle. We never analysed it. I suppose it was an oral cartoon. I read once that there were shades of Kafka, Ionesco and Dylan Thomas in it. Really it was just three blokes having a laugh, coupled with Spike's inventive genius.'

Recording **The Last Goon Show of All** brought back floods of nostalgia to all three. Secombe would like to do another series if it were possible to get all three of them in the same place at the same time, but Milligan thinks one show a year would be enough: 'This last programme didn't take long to write, but I wouldn't want to get involved in another series.'

Ray Ellington by Sellers

Spike's attitude towards the shows conflicts with that shared by both Sellers and Secombe. As the writer his role was paramount, and the strain told on him.

'The pressure and the tension of keeping up the standard drove me mad. I dedicated my whole life to it, seven days a week. Christ, it was terrifying. I used to get up, get to the BBC before nine, work right through

Harry Secombe by Sellers

the day and evening and get the last tube home. Sometimes I'd miss it and Peter would come and take me home in his car.

'It cost blood to put that show on for me. Sheer agony. It wrecked my first marriage and it wrecked my health. My nervous breakdown happened while I was on the show and I've been a neurotic ever since. So you can say I gave my sanity to that show.'

Says Secombe: 'All I remember is the constant hysteria and private jokes, like: "He's wearing a tenor's friend" – which was a truss with a spike attached. When we meet, anything else that has happened to us means nothing.'

And Peter Sellers: 'I can really say that it was the happiest professional period of my life. I never had such fun, enjoyment or fulfilment either before or since...' ●

GOONOLOGY

Sixty-nine programmes had been broadcast before the fourth Series of 1953, all untitled. This list does not include repeats.

Fourth Series

1953
2 October: The Dreaded Piano Clubber
9 October: The Destruction of England
16 October: The Everest Project
23 October: The Piano-Firing Cannon
30 October: The Gibraltar Story
6 November: The Sound Barrier Airing
    Cupboard
13 November: The First Albert Memorial to
    the Moon
20 November: The Missing Bureaucrat
27 November: Scradge
4 December: Alemain
11 December: Harry not a Dog
18 December: The Spanish Armada
25 December: The Giant Bombardon
1954
1 January: 10,000 Fathoms Down in a Wardrobe
8 January: 10 Downing Street Stolen
15 January: Dr Jekyll and Mr Crun
22 January: The Mummified Priest
29 January: A History of Communications
5 February: The Kippered Herring Gang
12 February: The Toothpaste Mines
15 February: The Case of the Vanishing Room
22 February: The Great Ink Drought of 1902
1 March: The Underwater Mountain
8 March: The Great Mustard & Cress Shortage
15 March: The Silent Bugler
22 March: Western Story
29 March: The Saga of the Internal Mountain
5 April: The Invisible Acrobat
12 April: The Great Bank of England Robbery
19 April: The Siege of Fort Knight
Fifth Series
31 August: The Starlings
28 September: The Whistling Spy Enigma
5 October: The Lost Goldmine of Charlotte

12 October: The Dreaded Batter Pudding Hurler
19 October: The Phantom Headshaver of
    Brighton
26 October: The Affair of the Lone Banana
2 November: The Canal
9 November: Lurgi Strikes Britain
16 November: The Mystery of the Marie Celeste
23 November: The Last Tram (from Clapham)
30 November: The Booted Gorilla
7 December: The Spanish Suitcase
14 December: Dishonoured
22 December: Frog
28 December: Ye Bandits of Sherwood Forest
1955
4 January: 1985
11 January: The Rightful Heir
18 January: The China Story
25 January: Under Two Floorboards – A Tale
    of the Legion
1 February: The Missing Scroll
15 February: The Sinking of Westminster Pier
22 February: The Fireball of Milton Street
1 March: The Terrible Blasting of Moreton's
    Bank
8 March: Yehti
15 March: The White Box of Great Bardsfield
22 March: The End (Confessions of a Secret
    Sennapods Drinker)
Sixth Series
20 September: The Man Who Won the War
27 September: The Secret Escritoire
4 October: The Lost Emperor
11 October: Napoleon's Piano
18 October: The Case of the Missing C.D.
    Plates
25 October: The Search for Rommel's Treasure
1 November: Foiled by President Fred
8 November: Lost Horizons
15 November: The International Christmas
    Pudding

22 November: The Hastings Flyer
29 November: The Sale of Manhattan
5 December: The Terrible Revenge of Fred
    Fu Manchu
13 December: The Lost Year
20 December: The Greenslade Story

1956

3 January: The Mighty Wurlitzer
10 January: The Red Bladder
17 January: Tales of Montmartre
24 January: The Guided Naaffi
31 January: The House of Teeth

7 February: Tales of Old Dartmoor.
14 February: The Choking Horror
21 February: The Tuscan Salami
28 February: The Treasure of Loch Lomond
1 March: Special St David's Day Programme
6 March: Fear of Wages
20 March: The Man Who Never Was
Seventh Series
4 October: The Bahrann Oasis
11 October: Drums along the Mersey
18 October: The Nadger Plague
25 October: The McReekie Rising of '74
1 November: The Spectre of Tinagel
8 November: The Sleeping Prince
22 November: Captain Seagoon RN
29 November: The Case of the Fake Neddie
    Seagoon
6 December: What's My Line
13 December: The Telephone
20 December: The Flea
27 December: Six Charlies in Search of an
    Author

1957

3 January: Bulldog Seagoon's First Case
10 January: Wings over Dagenham
17 January: The Rent Collectors
24 January: The Shifting Sands of Waziristan
31 January: The Moon Show
7 February: The Leather Omnibus
14 February: The Sleeping Prince
21 February: Round the World in 80 Days
28 February: Insurance, the White Man's Burden
6 March: The Trans-Africa Aeroplane Canal
13 March: I'll Meet by Goonlight
20 March: The Birmingham Ring Road
    Construction
27 March: The Histories of Pling the Elder
Eight Series
27 August: The Reason Why

30 September: The Spon Plague
7 October: The Junk Affair
14 October: Firechief Seagoon
21 October: The Great Regents Park Swim
28 October: The Treasure at the Tower
4 November: The Space Age
11 November: Rebellion at Red Fort
18 November: The Stolen Battleship
25 November: The Policy
2 December: King Solomon's Mines
9 December: The Stolen Postman
16 December: The Great British Revolution
23 December: The Plasticine Man
30 December: The Bridge on the River

1958

6 January: The Thing on the Mountain
13 January: The Great String Robberies
20 January: The Moriarty Murder Mystery
27 January: My Heart's in the Highlands
3 February: The White Neddie Trade
10 February: The Ten Snowballs That Shook
    The World
10 March: The TiddleyWinks Theft
17 March: The Lampost
24 March: The Great Statue Debate
Ninth Series
3 November: The Nude Welshman
10 November: I Was Monty's Treble
17 November: The Million Pound Penny
24 November: Pams Papers
1 December: The Mountain Eaters
8 December: King Arthur's Sword
15 December: Seagoon's Memoirs
22 December: Queen Anne's Reign
29 December: The Battle of Spion Kop

1959

5 January: Ned's Atomic Dustbin
12 January: The Spy
20 January: The Call of the West
2 February: The Scarlet Capsule
9 February: The Tay Bridge Disaster
16 February: The Gold-plate Robbery
23 February: The £50 Cure
Tenth Series
24 December: A Christmas Card
31 December: Tales of Men's Shirts

1960

7 January: Ned's Chinese Legs
14 January: Robins Past, A Story of Lord
    Seagoon
21 January: The Spanish Doubloons
28 January: The Last of the Smoking Seagoons

 # SPIKE MILLIGAN

Born in 1918 in India, where his father was a soldier, and came to England in 1934. Early jobs ranged from factory hand to scrubber in a laundry; he was also a trumpet player in a band for a while, then a trumpet player not in a band. He met Harry Secombe in the army, teamed up for concerts, began to write, met Peter Sellers – and so began the Goon Show.

HARRY SECOMBE

Born in 1921 in Wales, as a schoolboy he was already a popular 'turn' at church socials with his impersonations. After working as a pay clerk and completing war service, he took a job at the Windmill Theatre. It was there that he started to sing, and that the Sellers/Milligan/Bentine/Secombe association began.

PETER SELLERS

Born in 1925 into a family in which both parents and eight uncles were in show business. His career was a foregone conclusion, and after service in the RAF, he joined Ralph Reader's Gang Show. He then got a job at the Windmill, which soon led to recruitment by the BBC, and a remarkable film career, which began in 1954.

ALSO FEATURING:
Ray Ellington
An ex-RAF P.T. instructor, who formed his original Quartet in 1950.

Wallace Greenslade
Joined the staff of the BBC in 1945 as a general announcer, and worked on a wide variety of programmes until his death in 1961.

Max Geldray
Jazz harmonica player, he was born in 1916 in Holland, where he began his career. After many broadcasts in Europe, he settled in England after the war and began his radio and T.V. performances.

THE SCRIPTS

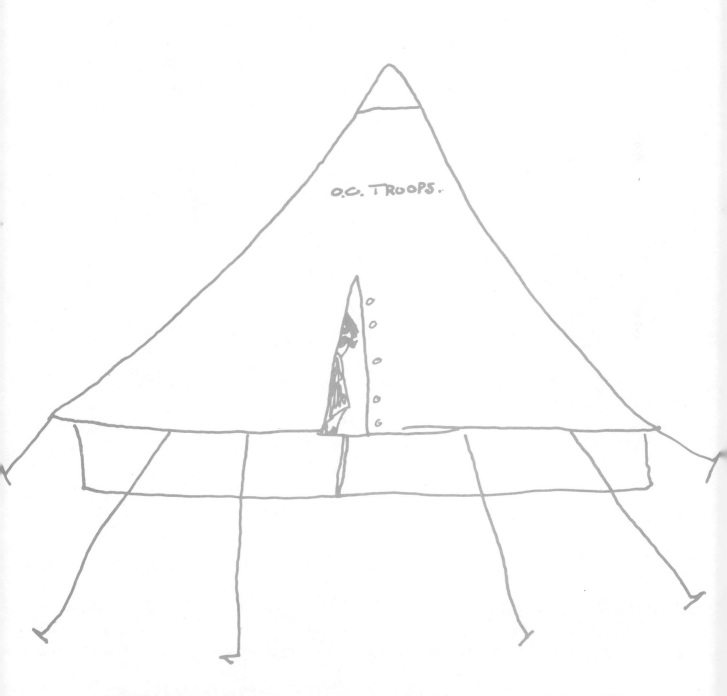

BATTLE OF SPION KOP

The Goon Show, No. 250 (9th Series, No. 9)
Transmission:
Monday, 29th December 1958: 8.30—9.00 p.m. Home Service
Wednesday, 31st December 1958: 9.30—10.00 p.m. Light Programme
Studio: Camden Theatre, London

Can England be saved by the British Army's rendition of 'Good-Bye Dolly I must leave you'? Will what saved Lord Nelson at Waterloo, likewise save Willium 'Mate' Cobblers from a fate worse than bananas? . . . . And is French Neddie's accent convincing? These and answers to other vital questions will not be revealed in the following pages. However, the full technicolour spectacle of British military dinners under fire, Bloodnok's secret woman receipe, and Moriarty's socks are here to be observed in microscopic detail, along with the full story of how the peaceful hamlet of Poknoips became the turbulent battleground of Spion Kop!

The main characters

Ned Seagoon	Harry Secombe
Major Denis Bloodnok	Peter Sellers
Captain Jympton	Spike Milligan
Eccles	Spike Milligan
Recruiting Sergeant	Harry Secombe
Moriarty	Spike Milligan
Grytpype-Thynne	Peter Sellers
Member of Parliament	Spike Milligan
Henry Crun	Peter Sellers
Minnie Bannister	Spike Milligan
Bluebottle	Peter Sellers
French Neddie	Harry Secombe
Moriarty-Bonaparte	Spike Milligan

The Ray Ellington Quartet
Max Geldray
Orchestra conducted by Wally Stott
Announcer: Wallace Greenslade
Script by Spike Milligan
Produced by John Browell

BATTLE OF SPION KOP

BILL	This is the BBC Light Programme. Now here is a variation on that. This is *the* BBC Light Programme.
OMNES & ORCHESTRA	**MURMURS OF APPROVAL**
PETER	The old night school's paying off there, Wal.
HARRY	Yer, chat on more on it there Wal lad.
BILL	I continue my recital of announcements. The BBC is open to the public on Thursdays and Wednesday afternoons, or, on Wednesday afternoons and Thursdays.
SPIKE	Thank you Jim, now here folks is Chief Ellinga to say Thursday in Swahali.
RAY	Ma ar la toola, yarga toola marngo, me ar gar tula la margu uta meel tick arrs fargoola tol dommmmmmmm . . .
SPIKE	You see how long the days are in Africa folks. Forward Mr Seaside with your New Year's resolutions.
SEAGOON	Thank you. Hello folks, hello folks, it is me folks. Next year folks I hope to give up 1958 permanently.
PETER	*(as elder statesman)* Ungrateful beast, after all 1958 has done for you, you discard it like an old boot, I won't hear it.
SEAGOON	Let me warn you hairy sir, of the many dangers and dongers of keeping on old years after it's worn out. Mrs Greenslade's husband will now tell you why.
BILL	It was the year 1907 and here is the orchestra to play it.
ORCHESTRA	**NEW MAD LINK ALL OVER THE SHOP. SINGING IN THE MIDDLE. SOUND F.X. IN MUSIC. FINISHES ON A CHORD.**
SEAGOON	Ohhh what a year that was . . . the South African war had broken out and was now in its second year.
OMNES & ORCHESTRA	**SING HAPPY BIRTHDAY —** *(fade)*
SEAGOON	Knock knock knock on a door in Africa.
BLOODNOK	Knock knock on a door in Africa . . . Gad, that's the address of my door — come in!
SEAGOON	Effects door opens . . .

BLOODNOK	Ahhh 'effects Ahhh'.
SEAGOON	May I introduce myself?
BLOODNOK	Of course.
SEAGOON	*(announcing)* Ladies and Gentlemen! The man in the blue corner is Neddie Seagoon.
SEAGOON	*(normal)* Thank you. I'm 5th Lieutenant Seagoon reporting from Sandhurst SW9.
BLOODNOK	Oh, sit down on that chair in Africa SE16.
F.X.	**DUCK CALL**
SEAGOON	Thank you. I was told to hand this envelope to you with a hand . . .
BLOODNOK	Oh . . . Pronounced . . .
GRAMS	**BLOODNOK Oooooooooooooh!!!**
F.X.	**ENVELOPE OPENING**
BLOODNOK	Oh, these are your secret orders.
SEAGOON	What do they say?
BLOODNOK	Standddddd Atttttt· . . . Ease . . .
GRAMS	**REGIMENT STANDING AT EASE**
SEAGOON	*(relief)* Oh, that feels much better sir.
BLOODNOK	Yes, and it suits you what's more. Now to military matters, of milt. Captain Jympton?
GRAMS	**MAD DAHS OF COCONUT SHELLS HORSES HOOVES VERY BRIEF, VERY FAST. APPROACHING TO FOREGROUND.**
JYMPTON	Ah *(stutters)* . . . sorry I'm late sir, I . . . was quelling a native with ah . . . quells.
BLOODNOK	You'll get the military piano and bar for this, ah . . . now explain the victorious positions of our defeated troops.
JYMPTON	Ah . . . intelligence ah . . . has established that the ah . . . people attacking us ar . . . are . . . are . . . the enemy.
BLOODNOK	So that's their fiendish game is it?
SEAGOON	Gentlemen, do the enemy realise that you have this information?
BLOODNOK	Oh no, we got 'em fooled, they think that *we're* the enemy.
SEAGOON	What a perfect disguise.
JYMPTON	Ha ha ha, yes you see Lieutenant Seagoon we have a plan — a plan of plin and ploof. The South Africans are magnificent fighters, and it's our intention to persuade them to come over to our side.
SEAGOON	Then that would finish the war sir!

JYMPTON	Oh no! Ha ha ha. Oh dearie no!
SEAGOON	Then how would you keep it going?
JYMPTON	England, my dear sir, is never short of enemies!
BLOODNOK	Of course not the waiting room's full of 'em. Now Seagoon, sit down, tell me what's the time back in England?

SEAGOON	Twenty to four sir.
BLOODNOK	Ah . . . it's nice to hear the old time again . . . Singhiz?
SINGHIZ	Yes sir?
F.X.	**SLAPSTICK**

BLOODNOK	Now get out will you! You see, Seagoon, how bad things are! That banana for instance . . . It's only been eaten once, and look at it!
SEAGOON	But sir, back in England they told me all was well.
BLOODNOK	Back in England, all *is* well. It's *here* where the trouble lies.
GRAMS	**EXPLOSION**
BLOODNOK	*(over above)* Oh — what the — eh — what?
GRAMS	**APPROACH OF OLD CAR BACK FIRING. GRINDING OF GEAR. PARPING ON BULB HORN. CAR EXPLODES . . . GUSHER OF STEAM. FALLS TO BITS . . . YELLS.**
ECCLES	Well . . . I think I'll pull-up here.
BLOODNOK	I say you . . . you with the apparent teeth.
ECCLES	Ohh a soldier . . . Hello soldier . . . Bang . . . Bang . . . Bang Bang . . . Bang — you're dead soldier!
SEAGOON	Let me talk to him. I speak Idiot fluently . . . *(does Eccles impression)* Hello Ecclesssss.
ECCLES	Oh? . . . You must be from the old country . . . Oh hohoh!
BLOODNOK	Neddie allow me to humour him with this mallet.
SEAGOON	No no no, leave it to me. *(as Eccles)* Tell us Mad Dan, wha' are you doing in Africa . . . Wha'n 'u doin' Africaaa . . .
ECCLES	'What are you doing in Africa' I translated. I'm here as an adviser to the British Army.
SEAGOON	*(as Eccles)* Splendid, what are you going to advise them?

ECCLES   Not to take me.

BLOODNOK   Oh, I respect your cowardice, it warms my heart and gives old Denis a real smart idea. Come over here and warm yourself by this Recruiting-Sergeant.

SERGEANT   *(cockney)* 'Ello 'ello 'ello my lad, you look a likely lad.

ECCLES   HELLO, hello, hello my laddddd. Yourn loonk linke a ohn *(rubbish)* . . .

SERGEANT   Very gude, very gude . . . 'ere lad, 'ow would you like to 'ave a grand-stand view of the opening night of the Battle of Spion Kop dere.

BLOODNOK   Just a moment sergeant . . . Spion Kop! He can have my place I tell you!

SERGEANT   Oh ho ho?

BLOODNOK   Yes, just by chance Sergeant I have a vacant uniform in the front rank, he'll see everything from there.

SERGEANT   Now then, you 'eard that very fair offer from the nice Major dere.

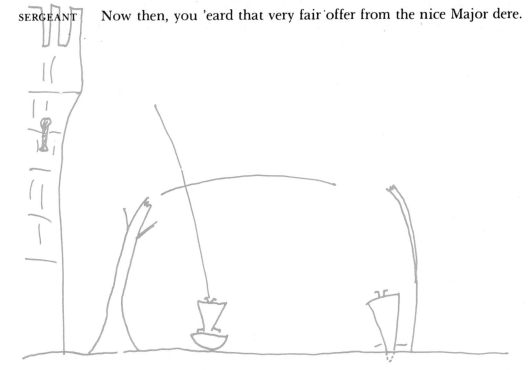

ECCLES   Yes, he's a nice Major — ah a nice man. How much do you want fer it?

BLOODNOK   Well, usually it's free, but just this once it will be seven shillings, so . . . ah shall we say a pound?

ECCLES   A pound?

BLOODNOK   You said it.

ECCLES   Oh . . . I've only got a five-pound note.

BLOODNOK   Well, I'll take that and you can pay me the other four later.

F.X.   **TILL**

BLOODNOK	Oh, the old Military till.
SERGEANT	You're a very lucky ladddd . . . . I'll have a regiment call for you at six tomorrow morning. Meantime here is the well known 'Conks' Geldray. A sittin' target.
MAX	Boy, in the war my conk holds its own.
MAX & ORCHESTRA	**MUSIC**

(applause)

ORCHESTRA	**DRAMATIC 'RETURN TO THE STORY' LINK (PRE-BATTLE)**
GRAMS	**HORSE ARTILLERY TROTTING UP THE LINE. DISTANT TRAMP OF SOLDIERS PLODDING ALONG ROUGH ROAD.**
BILL	At Dawn the British attack was mounted, not very well stuffed but beautifully mounted. And then suddenly through the stilled British front line, a lone voice is heard.
MORIARTY	*(approaching)* Lucky charms . . . get your lucky charms before the battle . . . get your lucky charmssssss. *(sings)* Get your self a charm today, and save yourself from harm today.
WILLIUM	'Ere . . . 'ere mate . . . charm man? 'Ere.
MORIARTY	What is it merry drummer man.
WILLIUM	Them charms, are they any cop mate?
MORIARTY	Ah, they're . . . they're real cop mate — Nelson bought one for Waterloo.
WILLIUM	He weren't at Waterloo.
MORIARTY	Of course not, he was in my shop buying a lucky charm. You see how lucky they are.
WILLIUM	How much is a good one then?
MORIARTY	Well certainly, what part don't you want to be wounded in?
WILLIUM	I don't want any of me parts wounded.
MORIARTY	I know, you want the all parts comprehensive charm.
WILLIUM	Hurry up then — how much??
MORIARTY	Three shillings, a bargain . . .
WILLIUM	THERE — I pins it on me chest so me chest won't get killed.
F.X.	**PISTOL SHOT**
WILLIUM	Owwwwwwwwwwwww Mateeeeeeeee.
F.X.	**THUD OF BODY**
MORIARTY	Good shot Grytpype.

GRYTPYPE-THYNNE	Unpin the lucky charm and back on the tray with it. Off you go.
MORIARTY	Charms, second hand lucky charms. *(fading)* Only used once . . .
GRYTPYPE-THYNNE	There he goes, a true son of France and Hyde Park. Who knows what mystic thoughts are whispering in the mossy glades of his krutty shins.
HARRY	*(hooray off)* I say, do you mind taking your hat off, old chap? The battle's about to begin, and we can't see you know.
GRAMS	**BATTLE STARTS — FIRST THE VOLLEYS OF MUSKETRY, THEN DISTANT CANNONS. THE RETURN FIRE OF THE ENEMY IS EVEN MORE DISTANT. FADE DOWN & UNDER. FADE IN BIG BEN CHIMING. FADE.**
ELDER STATESMAN	Gentlemen of the house, the Battle of Spion Kop opened last night.
OMNES & ORCHESTRA	**Here Here! Long Live the Empire!**
ELDER STATESMAN	Ahh, but I fear it got very bad notices in the Press.
M.P.	You're not thinking of taking it off are you, Mr Prime Minister?
ELDER STATESMAN	Well, unless Robert Morley puts some money in I can see no other way . . .
M.P.	But what about Binkie and his backers, they'll lose their money.
ELDER STATESMAN	Patience sir, patience. We have here Lieutenant Seagoon, who will proceed to give us the reason for the disaster.
SEAGOON	Thank you, Hon Members. The reason for it flopping was obvious . . . there isn't one decent song in the whole battle.
PETER	*(as another statesman)* But soldier fellow, the Battle of Spion Kop isn't musical!
SEAGOON	And that's where we went wrong. If the Americans had been running it they'd have had Rex Harrison, and the other wrecks.
ELDER STATESMAN	Do you know any good composers of battle scores?
SEAGOON	Just by chance and careful planning, I have an Auntie in Grimsby who sits among the cabbages and plays an elastic water tank under supervision.
ELDER STATESMAN	*(ecstatic)* I didn't know there were any of her kind left you know. Now off you go and tell your auntie the good news.
GRAMS	**RUNNING FOOTSTEPS & HARRY SINGS 'LAND OF HOPE AND GLORY' SPEEDING UP INTO THE DISTANCE.**
ORCHESTRA	**DRAMATIC CHORDS**
F.X.	**HAMMERING OF A METAL SPOON ON ANVIL**
CRUN	*(over hammering mutters)* Ohh, dear . . . there . . . now that's got the spoons in fine-spoons fettle Min.

F.X.	**QUICK TWO SPOONS TOGETHER A LA BUSKERS**
CRUN	*(sings)* 'Na ahah, ahah, ahah, ah' Now Min, get inside the piano and select me a tuning A.
GRAMS	**ONE SHEEP BLEATING**
CRUN	Again Min.
GRAMS	**ONE SHEEP BLEATING AGAIN**
CRUN	Oh, they don't make pianos like that any more.
MINNIE	Isn't it time we had it shorn Henery?
CRUN	No, not yet Min, the winters aren't upon us yet, you know. Hand me my knuckle oils.
MINNIE	Now Crun rub it well into the knuckles . . . it's mixed with Indian brandyyy.
BOTH	*(cries of brandyyy brandyyy).*
CRUN	Oh Min.
F.X.	**AGONISING KNUCKLE CRACKING**
CRUN	*(muttering over)* It's no good Min, I've got flat-feet in the third knuckle you know Min . . . Ah! . . . Ah well — Now to try for the Paganini variations for spoons arranged — Crun!!!!
GRAMS	**DISC OF VARIATIONS. CRUN PLAYS SPOONS AND WHISTLES.**
CRUN	Stop! Stop stop! This spoon is out of tune, Min. Have you been eating with it again?
MINNIE	No.
CRUN	*(power)* Then what's that your stirring the soup with?
MINNIE	A violin.
CRUN	She's always got an answer the old cow. Now to compose the last tune for the battle of Spion Kop.
F.X.	**BUSKER SPOONS IN TEMPO. MINNIE & CRUN SING 'DOLLY GREY' FADE.**
GRAMS	**FADE UP BATTLE NOISES. EXPLOSIONS. ETC.**
BLOODNOK	Aaaaaaaahhhh . . . aaahhh . . . ahhhhhhh. Ellinga . . . turn the volume of that battle down.
F.X.	**DOOR BURSTS OPEN**
SEAGOON	Major! The enemy are . . .
BLOODNOK	Aaahhhhh . . . Ah!
GRAMS	**WHOOSH**

SEAGOON	Good heavens, he's gone. Ah here are his boots, they're still warm he can't be far.
BLOODNOK	*(slightly off)* Aaahhh, there ain't nobody here but us chickens I tell you.
SEAGOON	The voice came from a cowardly red-face on the top of a chicken wardrobe.
BLOODNOK	Oh, it's you Seagoon, you you coward.
SEAGOON	Why have you deserted your post?
BLOODNOK	It's got woodworm sir.
SEAGOON	Old jokes won't save you.
BLOODNOK	They've saved Monkhouse and Goodwin, and that's good enough for me.
SEAGOON	Major, there's still hope. Crun's vital battle songs have arrived.
BLOODNOK	It won't be easy sir. The enemy have just attacked in E-Flat. And we had to retire to G-Minor.
SEAGOON	Never mind sir, these old songs are all written in six-sharps.
BLOODNOK	The most powerful brown key of them all. Get Ellinga and his Zulu bones to dash off a chorus towards the·enemy.
SEAGOON	Fire — !
RAY ELLINGTON QUARTET	**MUSIC** *(applause).*
ORCHESTRA	**DRAMATIC CHORDS**
GRAMS	**BUGLE CALL AT VARYINGPITCHES, MURMURS OF TROOPS TAKING UP POSITIONS.**

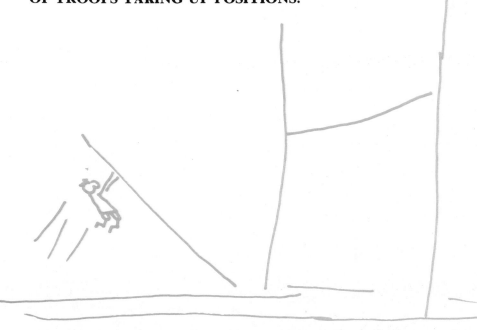

SEAGOON	At dawn under cover of daylight we took up our positions with our teeth blacked out.
SPIKE	*(woeful)* Every man has his ammunition pouches bulging with offensive military songs and spoons at the ready.
SEAGOON	**Right. We'll just have to sit and wait.** *(long pause)*
BLUEBOTTLE	You tink we're goin' to win, Captain?
SEAGOON	Never was victory more certain little lad.
BLUEBOTTLE	Oh . . . then why have you got that taxi waiting for you at the end of the trench.
SEAGOON	Ha ha . . . here's half-a-crown little lad. I think we can forget all about it now.
BLUEBOTTLE	No . . . I can't forget about it.
F.X.	**COLOSSAL CLOUT**
BLUEBOTTLE	Ahh . . . I forgotten about it.
SEAGOON	Now explain to me why you're lying down two-inches below the level of the ground and speaking through a tombstone.
BLUEBOTTLE	Well, I was dong an impression of a zebra crossing when . . . squelch! . . . a taxi ran over me breaking both my boots above the wrist.
SEAGOON	What agony igony ogony oogany mahogany . . . Did it hurt you?
BLUEBOTTLE	No because I'm making it all up. Ha hee . . .
SEAGOON	Taxi!
GRAMS	**TAXI APPROACHES AT TERRIFIC SPEED. JELLY THUD SOUND.**

BLUEBOTTLE	Oooh. You've taxied me. Look, the Christmas strings coming off my legs.
SEAGOON	Swallow this first-aid book and custard. I'll have your legs relacquered free and exported to Poland.
BLUEBOTTLE	You're a fair man, sir . . . Merry Krudmas.
ECCLES	Ooh, Bottle. What you doing under that taxi?
BLUEBOTTLE	It ran over me, Eccles.
ECCLES	You must be rich . . . I can only afford to be run over by buses.
BLUEBOTTLE	Well my man when you're in the big money you know, you can do things like this.
ECCLES	You see, one day I'll have enough money to be run over by a Rolls-Royce with a chauffeur.
BLUEBOTTLE	Well, pull me out then.
ECCLES	Right. Hold this.
BLUEBOTTLE	What is it?
ECCLES	I don't know, but I got it cheap.
SEAGOON	Let me see what you got cheap?
GRAMS	**TIGER GROWL**
SEAGOON	Good heavens it's a genuine hand operated 1914 tiger!
BLOODNOK	Seagoon, put that tiger back in its stripes . . . we don't want any scandals during ladies night.
JYMPTON	Pardon me, sir. All the men are ready with their music.
BLOODNOK	Good, let's have those spoons then lad.
ORCHESTRA	**EACH MAN ISSUED WITH TWO SPOONS. THEY MAKE NOISE LIKE BUSKERS.**
BLOODNOK	Oooh . . . what a terrifying sound. It's a good job nobody heard it.
SEAGOON	Now men, to your military Crun music and take up your vocal positions with your voices facing outwards.
BLOODNOK	And don't sing men until you see the whites of their song sheets. Bugler, sound the elephant.
GRAMS	**INFURIATED HIGH PITCHED TRUMPETING BY SINGLE ELEPHANT**
BLOODNOK	Ohhh . . .
JYMPTON	Here they come now, sir.
BLOODNOK	Quick, me spoons and me music. I'll show 'em . . .
F.X.	**TWO SPOONS BUSKING IN TEMPO TO BLOODNOK SINGING 'GOODBYE DOLLY I MUST LEAVE YOU'**

BLOODNOK	'Goodbye Dolly, I must leave you.' *(shouts)* Come on you fools, there's more where that came from. *(continues singing)* 'Off we go and fight the foe.' *(shouts)* Sing up lads!
OMNES & ORCHESTRA	**ALL JOIN IN SINGING AND RATTLING SPOONS**
GRAMS	**SHELLS START BURSTING IN THEIR MIDST. STARTING SLOWLY & INCREASING IN INTENSITY. BLOODNOK CONTINUES TO SING BUT GRADUALLY HIS MORALE IS DESTROYED. HE BREAKS OFF.**
BLOODNOK	Run for it lads . . . Oooh, these songs aren't bullet proof.
GRAMS	**WHOLE ARMY RUNS AWAY YELLING IN TERROR. SPEED UP AND FADE.**
	(pause)
GRAMS	**ARCTIC GALE HOWLING. OCCASIONAL WOLVES. THEN APPROACH OF RUNNING ARMY STILL YELLING & PANTING. ALL GRADUALLY SLOW DOWN BY SLOWING RECORD.**
BLOODNOK	That's far enough lads, where are we?

SEAGOON	The South Pole sir.
BLOODNOK	No further, we don't want to back into them. Oh . . . plant the Union Jack will you? The national flag of the Union of Jacks. I claim the South Pole in the name of Gladys Ploog of 13 The Sebastibal Villas, Sutton.
SEAGOON	Who is she, sir?
BLOODNOK	I don't know, but obviously we're doing her a big favour.
SEAGOON	There's still a chance of victory. Look what I've got in the brown paper parcel.
F.X.	**RUSTLING OF PAPER**
BLOODNOK	Good heavens white paper, what a glorious victory for England.
SEAGOON	Look under the stamp.
BLOODNOK	What? A fourteen-inch naval gun.
ECCLES	And guess what's in the barrel?
BLOODNOK	I've no idea.
SEAGOON	Major, inside the barrel are photographs of a British military dinner.

BLOODNOK	Really . . . Keep it going lads, keep it going.
SEAGOON	I intend to fire that photograph at the enemy canteen during their lunch break. When they see the size of British military dinners they'll desert.
BLOODNOK	I know . . . half our men deserted when they saw the size of 'em. However it's worth a try. Take aim . . . fire!
GRAMS	**COLOSSAL EXPLOSION. FOLLOWED BY PILES OF BONES FALLING ON TO THE GROUND.**
BLUEBOTTLE	Ah . . . that's the last time I kip in a barrel. Collapses, and is left out of show from now onwards. Goodnight everybody.
GRAMS	**CHEERS APPLAUSE**
BLUEBOTTLE	Oh . . . by popular request I come back again.
F.X.	**SLAPSTICK**
BLUEBOTTLE	Ahhh . . .
SEAGOON	All we can do is to wait and see what effect that photograph of a military dinner has on the enemy. Meantime a sound effect.
GRAMS	**WIND UP AND WOLVES HOWLING**
BILL	Meantime in Parliament the British Government had written off the Battle of Spion Kop as a dead loss.
HARRY	*(statesman)* Gentlemen, um, um . . . to save face and the honour of England, we're going to bring back that old favourite um, ah . . . the Battle of Waterloo.

OMNES & **ORCHESTRA**	**ANCIENT MURMURS OF APPROVAL**
ELDER STATESMAN	Gentlemen, we shall send out immediate notification to the original cast.
ORCHESTRA	**MARSEILLAISE-TYPE LINK**
MORIARTY BONAPARTE	*(snoring).*
F.X.	**DOOR OPENING**
FRENCH NEDDIE	Mon Emperor, wake-up!
MORIARTY BONAPARTE	How dare you wake the Emperor Napoleon up in the middle of his retirement.
FRENCH NEDDIE	Wonderful news . . . by special request we have to do an encore of the Battle of Waterloo.
MORIARTY BONAPARTE	What . . . but we lost it.
FRENCH NEDDIE	This time we've got a British backer.
MORIARTY BONAPARTE	Get my trousers oiled and unwrap a fresh Josephine . . . ahh, there's going to be fun tonight.
F.X.	**THWACK**
GRYTPYPE-THYNNE	Down Emperor down . . . back to your grave. You know you're not allowed out after your death.
MORIARTY BONAPARTE	Blast these silly rules.
GRYTPYPE-THYNNE	My card Neddie.

SEAGOON	This is a piece of string.
GRYTPYPE-THYNNE	Have you no imagination lad. I am Lord Ink.
SEAGOON	Not Pennan?
GRYTPYPE-THYNNE	Yes Pennan Ink.
ORCHESTRA	**CHORD IN C**
SEAGOON	Don't worry folks, it's getting near the end now. All pay offs will be gratefully received.
GRYTPYPE-THYNNE	One coming up, Ned. Unfortunately my client Moriarty is appearing in 'The Death of Napoleon' at the local nackers yard . . . it looks like being a very long run.
SEAGOON	It looks like being a long run? What does?
GRYTPYPE-THYNNE	Ten miles.
F.X.	**PISTOL SHOT**
GRAMS	**TWO PAIRS OF RUNNING FEET**
SEAGOON	*(panting)* As we ran we discussed the contract for the Battle of Waterloo. Later at Preston Barracks Brighton, we auditioned for the part of the Duke of Wellington.
GRAMS	**FADE IN PETER SINGING LAST PART OF 'ANY OLD IRON' MATE**
SEAGOON	Thank you. Wait inside the piano one moment will you. What do you think?
GRYTPYPE-THYNNE	He's not the Lord Wellington type you know.
SEAGOON	Yes. *(calls out)* I say — we'll write and let you know.
WILLIUM	Let me know what?
SEAGOON	That you're no good for the part.
WILLIUM	Rite — I won't take another job till I hear that, then.
SEAGOON	Next please.
ECCLES	*(sings)* I'll follow my secret heart till I find you . . .
SEAGOON	One moment. *(aside)* Where's my pistol?
GRYTPYPE-THYNNE	No Neddie no one moment . . .
MORIARTY BONAPARTE	Grytpype . . . with Eccles playing the part of Wellington this time the French are bound to win the battle of Waterloo.
GRYTPYPE-THYNNE	Right . . . Eccles? Button the hat and sword. Now Charge . . .
GRAMS	**GREAT GALLOPING OF HORSES INTO DISTANCE WITH SHOTS SCREAMS AND MORE SHOTS**
SEAGOON	*(in tears)* No . . . we've . . . we've lost the Battle of Waterloo.

MORIARTY	New history books . . . get your new history books here . . . read all the truth about Waterloo.
F.X.	**PHONE RINGS**
SEAGOON	Hello?
BLOODNOK	Seagoon, look here, a right twitt you made of yourself firing that photo of a dinner at the enemy. Do you know what they've fired back?
SEAGOON	What?
BLOODNOK	The photograph of an empty plate.
SEAGOON	Well, there you are folks the old anti-climax again.
ORCHESTRA	**'OLD COMRADES MARCH' PLAYOUT**

NED'S ATOMIC DUSTBIN

The Goon Show, No. 251 (9th Series, No. 10)
Transmission:
Monday, 5th January 1959: 8.30—9.00 p.m. Home Service
Wednesday, 7th January 1959: 9.30—10.00 p.m. Light Programme
Studio: Camden Theatre, London

Another explosive drama of espionage and futility, in which the British Government is nearly overthrown by a security leek. Mrs Gladys Smith, the doubtful heroine, is disguised both as Major Denis Bloodnok and 'Mad Dan' Eccles and infilthtrated into the Russian Secret Service. Under her code-name Bluebottleski, she prevents single-handed the Russian sabotage of Neddie's atomic dustbin. Her escape over the Vulgar Rapids, with the prototype strapped to her Union Jack underwear, was later classified as unfit for children. This story has been previously dramatised by Newton Abbot Wolf-Cubs, and is now moored off Portsmouth Point.

The main characters

Ned Seagoon	Harry Secombe
Minnie Bannister	Spike Milligan
Henry Crun	Peter Sellers
Lord Scradds	Spike Milligan
Cynthia Fruit	Peter Sellers
Grytpype-Thynne	Peter Sellers
Moriarty	Spike Milligan
Willium	Peter Sellers
Prime Minister	Peter Sellers
Minister Fred	Harry Secombe
Minister Monty	Spike Milligan
Lord Stron	Spike Milligan
Comrade Spottovitch	Spike Milligan
Comrade Spondovitch	Peter Sellers
Comrade Toolsvitch	Harry Secombe
Bluebottle	Peter Sellers
Eccles	Spike Milligan
Major Denis Bloodnok	Peter Sellers

The Ray Ellington Quartet
Max Geldray
Orchestra conducted by Wally Stott
Announcer: Wallace Greenslade
Script by Spike Milligan
Produced by John Browell

NED'S ATOMIC DUSTBIN

BILL   This is the BBC Light Programme. To add seasonal cheer to the broadcast I have had written permission to wear a small holly leaf in my button hole.

SEAGOON   Don't you realise Wal boy, that the Druids used the holly leaf for certain unsavoury ritualistic rites.

BILL   Oh dear, well I'd better hurry and get that word cleared by the BBC censorship department. Gid up there!

GRAMS   **HORSES GALLOP OFF VERY FAST**

F.X.   **KNOCK ON DOOR**

HARRY   (*older than God*) Ahhh . . . mara . . . ahh comeee . . . ahhhh . . . ahhh . . . ahhhhhhh.

MINNIE   He's trying to say 'come in'.

CRUN   Male hormones forever! Ahhh . . . hha (*collapses*) Ahhhhh . . . mr . . .

F.X.   **THUD OF BODY & BITS OF BODY SCATTERING.**
BALL BEARINGS MARBLES ROLL ALONG FLOOR.
HAND FULL OF FORKS. METALLIC RESONANT
NUTS & BOLTS FALLING.

CRUN   Oh dear he's disinteregated Min . . . I'll have to take over his trousers.

F.X.   **DOOR OPENS. GALLOPING HOOVES AT GREAT`**
SPEED (COCONUT SHELLS).

BILL   Ahoy . . . I've come to get clearance on a word.

CRUN   What is the word, sir?

BILL   Well its er um . . . um. Yes . . . 'Holly'!

CRUN   What's wrong with it sir?

BILL   Well it is believed to have undertones of eroticism.

CRUN   Oh Dear . . .

MINNIE   Ohhh.

CRUN   Could you write this word down?

MINNIE   Blindfold yourself Henery, don't look!

BILL   Yes . . . I could.

F.X.	**WRITING**
GRAMS	**LOUD STARTLED CLUCK OF CHICKEN . . .**
CRUN	*(aside)* Blast! He can write on chickens. You want us to see if this word is fit to be said?
BILL	I fear so.
CRUN	Ohh dear, well that puts us in a rather nasty spot doesn't it. We don't like committing ourselves.
BILL	But you're the Censors.
CRUN	Ah but we don't like that sort of thing. We don't do it.
HARRY	*(Yorkshire)* Mr Lord Scradds, you're the oldest, what do you think of this word?
LORD SCRADDS	Ahhhhh . . . ahhhh, ahh I'll I won't commit myself at this ahhhhhhhhh at this stage . . . I . . . I'll . . . go along Yes . . . I . . . I'll go along . . .
CRUN	Who will you go along with?
SPIKE	Ahhhhh, anybody a . . .
PETER	*(Aussie)* I think I'm with you there, I'm with you all the way, I'll go along with that.
SPIKE	*(Hooray)* I ratar mark the omplication the most of the marn arve bwin time waste and non the far the plo Car there at Dawn.
CRUN	Ha ha ha you devil you devil . . . you devil . . . So then it's agreed that we all agree? Now what was the question?
BILL	The word 'holly', is it — ?
MINNIE	Canteen's open!
OMNES	**SCREAMS OF 'TEAAAAAAA' . . .**
GRAMS	**GREAT RUSH OF BOOTS DEPARTING. DISTANT SLAMMING DOORS VERY FAST . . .**
SEAGOON	Well, well, well they've escaped under cover of stupidity. Forward Tar Plee ti Pinggeee.
PETER	It is I, Tom.
SEAGOON	Yes, it's old 'it is I Tom', Peter Sellers — playboy of Old Finchley tube station and friend of West End managements.
PETER	I see a vision, Tom.
SEAGOON	Well, hold this song and accompany this next announcement.
PETER	*(sings idiot tunes behind Bill)*
BILL	Ladies and Gentlemen, what kind of Christmas has it been. Let us recount one, two, three. *(fade)*
GRAMS	**ECCLES SINGING 'GOOD KING WENCESLAS'. (THE CHORAL ONE).**

SPIKE   Hello, Terry Frulls here and we're going over now to the Services Station in the Christmas Islands, over to them.

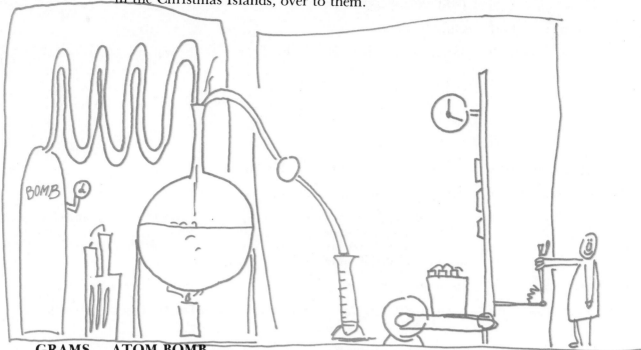

GRAMS   **ATOM BOMB...**

HARRY   (*kid*) Look Mum, another Atom Bomb.

PETER   (*mum*) You lucky boy, that means Daddy will be home early from work.

SEAGOON   Here in London we interview passers by . . . Excuse me, sir, do you believe in a White Christmas?

RAY   Are you kidding?

SEAGOON   Ha ha ha and . . . and you, madam, do you believe in an old fashioned Christmas by the fire?

PETER   (*whoops dear*) Oh, not harf dear.

SEAGOON   Conks? Play that arrangement for nose and harmonica, me? I'm for the old brandy there.

GRAMS   **GREAT RUSH OF RECEDING BOOTS...**

MAX & ORCHESTRA   **MUSIC**

(*applause*)

BILL   Tar Tar . . . Thank you. Now over Christmas a great story broke, being no newspapers it missed the headlines, but here it is in all it's monkey para toot toot pin pon pee pee peee, tiddley. I doe too is the Story of the Tun tack tock!

ORCHESTRA   **DRAMATIC CHORDS...**

SPIKE   It is Christmas and somewhere in a goatskin flat in naughty Wales, a young hairy titch is working on a painting of a painting!

SEAGOON	(*fade in*) (*sings*) I painted here, IIIII painted here ha ha ha, now a dab of red here and a touch of puce, here.
CYNTHIA FRUIT	Ohhhh!
SEAGOON	Steady Miss Fruit, keep still . . .
CYNTHIA FRUIT	It's awfully cold posing like this.
SEAGOON	I've got the candle on! Now, there! There we are, you can relax. It's a masterpiece.
CYNTHIA FRUIT	What is it.
SEAGOON	The plans of a new British dustbin.
CYNTHIA FRUIT	And you've had me posing nude for that?
SEAGOON	It's something to do with my unhappy childhood. Off you go and change behind that glass screen . . . ah! There she goes, T.V. was never like this . . . Knok, knik knack knock knockitty knokck knock knock . . . It's an impression of a door knocker. Come in!
CRUN	Impression of Innn.
SEAGOON	Steaming Pud, it's me old wrinkled retainer Uncle Crun in his new King-size nightshirt.
GRAMS	**WHOOSH OF WIND**
CRUN	Ohhhhhhhhh.
SEAGOON	I wonder where that draught's coming from.
CRUN	I don't know where it's coming from but I know where it's going. Ah ah ah ah ah Christmas Cracker Joker!
GRAMS	**WHOOSH OF WIND AGAIN. (AS BEFORE) . . .**
CRUN	Ohhhhhhhhh . . . this nightshirt is too big for me, the wind is . . .
SEAGOON	Wait, there's another pair of legs sticking out of the bottom.
CRUN	Ohhhh, who's that in there, come out of I'll . . .
ECCLES	No I'll come out, 'ello Neddie, 'ello Uncle Crun . . . 'ello, I been slummin'.
SEAGOON	Eccles, what you doing in that nightshirt?
ECCLES	Nuttin'. Everythings marked 'don't touch'.
CRUN	Antiques, you know. But how did you get in? That's what I want to know.
ECCLES	I got a map of your legs.
SEAGOON	Come on out at once.
F.X.	**DOOR OPENS**
SEAGOON	A door in the nightshirt opened and out stepped a street with a man in it.
GRYTPYPE-THYNNE	I say, what is all this noise? There's people in that nightshirt trying to sleep you know.

SEAGOON	What what what . . . you'll get a biff on the knee. Explain that Krutty hand operated mattress.
GRYTPYPE-THYNNE	That mattress Sir, contains the princely string and nut-bound body of such stuff as steams are made of, none other than the Count Jim 'Wakey Wakey' . . .
F.X.	**COLOSSAL SLAP ON BARE SKIN (SLAP STICK) . . .**
GRYTPYPE-THYNNE	. . . Moriarty.
F.X.	**SCRATCHING**
MORIARTY	Owwwww . . . greetings my loyal subjects and —
F.X.	**SLAPSTICK**
GRYTPYPE-THYNNE	Stop that revolting scratching will you Count. The dear Count is plagued this year with a return of the Royal Strains.
SEAGOON	Does he really own that nightshirt.
GRYTPYPE-THYNNE	Yes. 'een now, see how he walks the battlements . . . Of course he only rents the top.
SEAGOON	What about the rents in the bottom?
GRYTPYPE-THYNNE	Ned, old jokes will get you nowhere. Look what it did to the Count.
SEAGOON	Oh, I apologise for my altitude.
GRYTPYPE-THYNNE	It is low, Ned, could we sell you an extra three feet?
SEAGOON	Just what I need.
GRYTPYPE-THYNNE	Moriarty, saw three feet off your wooden leg.
MORIARTY	No, I'm going to the ball as a toffee apple.
GRYTPYPE-THYNNE	It's for money!
F.X.	**FURIOUS SAWING. END DROPS OFF.**
GRYTPYPE-THYNNE	There Ned, three feet.
F.X.	**TILL**
SEAGOON	Thank you. I'll tie it to my head and put my hat on it.
MORIARTY	Ohh Sapristi! He looks like . . .
GRYTPYPE-THYNNE	Don't tell him!
SEAGOON	Now I must get my plans of the dustbin up to London. Where's the nearest station?
GRYTPYPE-THYNNE	In this cupboard. Admission 3d.
F.X.	**TILL. CUPBOARD DOOR OPENS.**
GRAMS	**STATION**
WILLIUM	'Ere. Shut that door will yer . . . you want me train to catch cold?

SEAGOON	When's the next one to London town devine?
WILLIUM	Arsk that hairy doggie over der.
SEAGOON	Does he speak?
WILLIUM	Does he what? Does he speak? — 'ere listen, listen to this. 'Ello dog, 'ello doggie, go on tell 'im doggie . . . No, he don't speak.
SEAGOON	How does he know when the train goes?
WILLIUM	I told 'im. Ohh! I can feel a low stabbin' pain in the seams of me underpants. That means it's 9.20! Time to go in it . . . Hold tight.
F.X.	**GUARDS WHISTLE**
GRAMS	**TRAIN WHISTLE. THEN HORSE CLOPS SLOWLY AWAY.**
SEAGOON	Bit short of coal aren't you?
WILLIUM	Yer, you ain't got a bit on you ave you?
SEAGOON	No, I gave up carrying it.

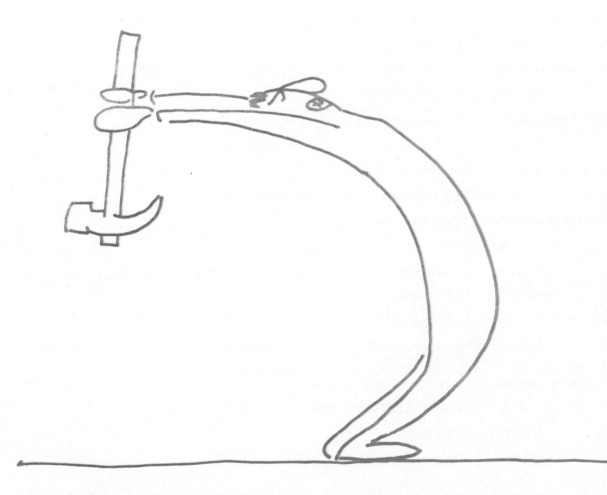

WILLIUM	Cor, taking chances eh?
BILL	On arrival in London town devine, Neddie rushed to 10 Downing Street.
F.X.	**KNOCK ON DOOR. DOOR OPENS.**
RAY	(*African chief*) What you want man?
SEAGOON	Here, who are you?
RAY	I'm the Foreign Secretary, man.
SEAGOON	Yes, you do look a bit foreign.
RAY	Oh steady man, that could mean war with Ghana.
PRIME MINISTER	I say Bazil, who is that blotting out the sun with his head?
RAY	It's a man with a wooden leg tied to his nut with a hat on top.
PRIME MINISTER	Oh, that'll be Lord Hailsham, I expect.
SEAGOON	No sir, I'm Ned Seagoon. I've got plans.
PRIME MINISTER	Eh? Let's have a look.
F.X.	**UNROLLING PLANS**
PRIME MINISTER	Nothing here.
SEAGOON	The drawings on the other side.
PRIME MINISTER	Oh, that's a clever idea, who'd have guessed? Ahhhh live and learn . . . plans of new anti-atomic dustbin . . . Ohhh.
SEAGOON	Yes, you see, in the event of radiation, this dustbin will keep your garbage atom free.
PRIME MINISTER	What rubbish!
SEAGOON	Indeed.
PRIME MINISTER	Well, here's a CBE on account. Now, would you like to try for the Knight-star and Garter?
SEAGOON	If it's okay with you sir, it's alright with me.
PRIME MINISTER	Good. Come back tomorrow with Hughie Green. Until then a sailor's farewell.
GRAMS	**SPLASH**
F.X.	**DOOR SLAMS**
PRIME MINISTER	I say, what an ideal intro for Rain Elungton.
RAY ELLINGTON QUARTET	**MUSIC**

(*applause*)

47

BILL	Hardly had that music ceased and the wind gone up the chimney, when the Prime Minister presented the new atom-proof dustbin to a meeting of high-ranking idiots.
GRAMS	**SHEEP**
PRIME MINISTER	Gentlemen, this dustbin has great potential, potontial and putuntial.
MINISTER FRED	Can it go to the moon?
PRIME MINISTER	No, but from small beginnings y'know, what what.
MINISTER MONTY	Is this the prototype?
PRIME MINISTER	No, that is the dustbin.
F.X.	**LID OF BIN LIFTED UP AND DOWN**
MINISTER MONTY	It sounds like a dustbin.
F.X.	**DUSTBIN**
PRIME MINISTER	(*sudden boyish interest*) I say, may I try that?
F.X.	**DUSTBIN SOUND A LITTLE MORE EAGER**

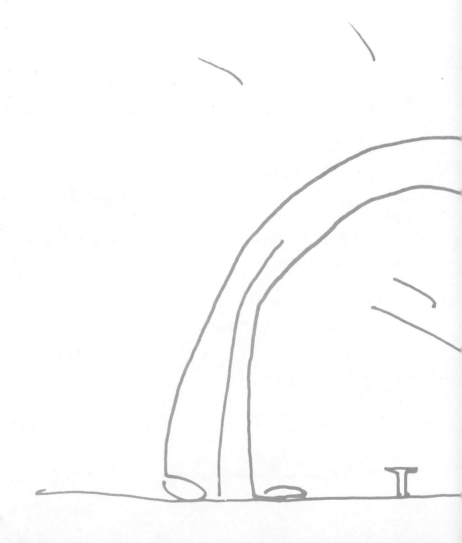

PRIME MINISTER	Ha ha ha — I say it's not difficult at all, is it?
F.X.	**DUSTBIN AS ABOVE**
HARRY	*(ageing)* Let . . . I say fellas . . . let me try now.
F.X.	**DUSTBIN DIFFERENT TEMPO TO DENOTE THAT SOMEONE ELSE HAS TAKEN OVER**
HARRY	*(ageing)* Oh ha ha ha oh dear, oh dear, why didn't we get one of these before, eh?
PRIME MINISTER	Now me again.
F.X.	**DUSTBIN**
OMNES	**ALL LAUGH, EXCITED NOISES ABOUT BANGING THE BIN**
F.X.	**ADD DUSTBIN TO THE ABOVE LAUGHTER**
	(the above extended)
PRIME MINISTER	Yes, ahem, now Lord Stron, tell the House of your plan.

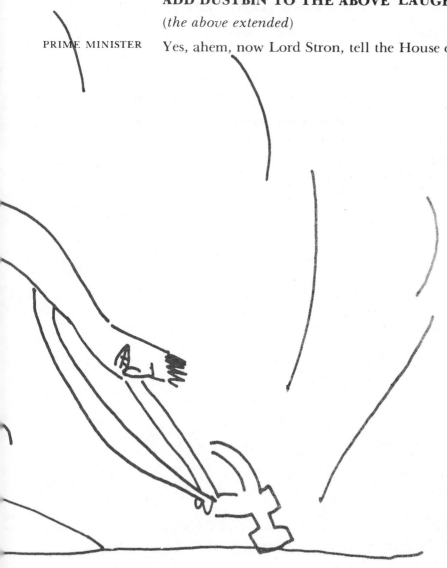

LORD STRON	Yes, we intend to find if it's possible for a man to go over the Niagara Falls in this dustbin. *(cries of here here)* We've got to keep it pretty dark, otherwise the Russians will start putting dustbins into orbit on the Volga rapids. Gentlemen, if you'll all step into this train . . .
F.X.	**SOUND OF IRON BAR CLANGING**
BILL	Believe it or not, that was the sound of the Kremlin.
SPOTTOVITCH	Comrade Spondervitch, there is a man outside to see you.
SPONDOVITCH	Comrade Toolsvitch, send him in.
TOOLSVITCH	Come in, son of Mata Hari.
F.X.	**DOOR OPENS**
GRAMS	**SERIES OF FAST APPROACHING FOOTSTEPS**
BLUEBOTTLE	The Black Eagle is sitting on the Red Flower Pot.
TOOLSVITCH	The password!
BLUEBOTTLE	Oh? All is well. Comrades, Bluebottleski is here with cardboard to spare.
SPOTTOVITCH	Tell us Comrade, what kind of undercover work have you done?
BLUEBOTTLE	*(naughty)* Ohh, I cannot tell that. Oh, I don't know though . . . Well I was look-out for the Finchley Wolf Cubs.

TOOLSVITCH	(*keen*) Ahh, what did you spot?
BLUEBOTTLE	I spotted Mrs Evans and the Milkman.
TOOLSVITCH	What did you get for that?
BLUEBOTTLE	A clout on my ear 'ole.
TOOLSVITCH	There is a tin rouble, get the plans of the British anti-atomic dustbin . . . or you will lose your deposits.
ECCLES	What's goin' on here.
TOOLSVITCH	Who are you?
ECCLES	Stalin.
F.X.	**PISTOL SHOT**
ECCLES	Owwwwwww!
BLUEBOTTLE	You twitt, Ecclesavitch. Come wid me . . . farewell comrades. Nothing but death can stop Bottleski from the plans. Farewell.
F.X.	**DOOR SLAMS . . . DOOR OPENS**
BLUEBOTTLE	Here, dere's a big spider out dere, Oh!
ECCLES	I ain't frightened of big spiders. I'll fix him.
F.X.	**DOOR SLAMS**
GRAMS	**TERRIBLE BATTLE. ECCLES YELLING FOR HELP. THUDS BANGS ETC GREAT ROARING OF A LION AROUSED.**
F.X.	**DOOR SLAMS**
BLUEBOTTLE	'Ere where's all your clothes?
ECCLES	Bottle, say after me, I must learn the difference between a lion and a spider.
BLUEBOTTLE	Ohh . . . ah ha.
ORCHESTRA	**DRAMATIC LINK**
SEAGOON	Hello folks, Neddie here folks; meantime the plans went ahead to test my dustbin over the Niagara Falls. For this the Government brought the Niagara Falls to London and put it up at the Savoy. In charge was a master of nuclear explosions.
ORCHESTRA	**LAST PART OF BLOODNOK THEME**
GRAMS	**BOMBS EXPLODING ETC**
BLOODNOK	Ohhhhhh. It's a good job the room's sound proof, poor Frank Sinatra upstairs, my goodness.
GRAMS	**ATOM BOMB**

BLOODNOK	Oh, that was the best explosion of the series.
SEAGOON	Was it Christmas Island?
BLOODNOK	No, Christmas pudding.
SEAGOON	Oh, grand news. We have managed to send an elephant up the Falls in the atomic-proof dustbin, and it lived.
BLOODNOK	What? No other dustbin has ever done it and lived.
SEAGOON	Now next, we want a human being to go in it.
BLOODNOK	We'll draw lots for it now. Eccles, write your name on fifty pieces of paper, and put them in a hat.
ECCLES	Right, dere.
BLOODNOK	Now, draw it out. What's it say?
ECCLES	Mrs Gladys Smith.
BLOODNOK	You imposter . . . you're not Mrs Gladys Smith, I am!
ECCLES	I don't want to die.
BLOODNOK	You don't want to die, you superstitious fool, you superstitious mule you . . . You won't die Eccles. Roll up your trousers!

GRAMS   **WOODEN SLAT BLIND PULLED UP**

BLOODNOK	Ohhhh . . . just as I thought, legs that reach the ground. Now strap him in that dustbin for the test.
ECCLES	No no, let me go! Take your filthy hand off my filthy arm I . . .
ORCHESTRA	**DRAMATIC CHORDS**
GRAMS	**JOHN SNAGGE: This is London calling in the uncut bicycle service of the Ba Be See. This afternoon, the Prime Minister, told an eager half-empty House that today, England would launch an atomic dustbin into the Niagara Falls, with a highly qualified pilot at the controls. There were demonstrations at the dustbin launching base, when a million barber electricians carrying soup tureens laid down in the road, with socks full of grit. The driver of the steam roller said 'It was so tempting, I'm sorry, I won't do it again' . . . Arsenal 8 — Tottenham 87 . . .** (fade)
GRYTPYPE-THYNNE	Hear that Neddie? They're debasing the original use of your dustbin.
SEAGOON	I'll get my revenge.
MORIARTY	No, I'll get mine.
SEAGOON	No no no, thank you, but my revenge is stronger and it lasts the whole drink through.

GRYTPYPE-THYNNE	Ned, for no reason at all, I will become your solicitor. Take a letter on uncut lino. 'Dear Bloodnok . . .
F.X.	**NAILING DOWN LINO. CONTINUES UNDER DICTATION.**
GRYTPYPE-THYNNE	Unless you return the plans of Ned's dustbin, I will be forced to charge my client a higher rate.' Signed Thynne. Now let me hear that back.
GRAMS	**THYNNE: 'SIGNED THYNNE' PLAYED A LITTLE FASTER.**
GRYTPYPE-THYNNE	Splendid. Now, go and lay that under his military kippers.
SEAGOON	Ha ha ha, he who laffs liffs loofs las, ahem; he who har hees, laffs loose lifs. Hee farewell.
GRAMS	**WHOOSH**
SEAGOON	Bloodnok!
BLOODNOK	Ohhhhhh!
SEAGOON	Ha ha this lino means curtains for you.
BLOODNOK	Lino curtains? What a quaint seasonal custom . . . wait, this is solicitors lino. You'll hear from my linoleum layer in the morning sir. Meantime, take that!
GRAMS	**JELLY SPLOSH**
SEAGOON	What is it?
BLOODNOK	I don't know sir. It was dark when I trod in it.
SEAGOON	Gad, it's a banner with a strange device, and clutched by a lad in snow and ice.
BLUEBOTTLE	Get your hands up.
SEAGOON	Bluebottle, take that silly rice-paper off.
BLUEBOTTLE	You touch one hair of dat and Sflaishiou! The disingrater ray gun will speak in my hand, ha ah ha.
F.X.	**CLANG**
BLUEBOTTLE	Oh, the 'lastic's come off the trigger.
SEAGOON	Don't cry Bottle, here, have the suspender off my sock.
BLUEBOTTLE	Oh thanks . . . no . . . no! That suspender is just a glittering Western prize to make me forget my mission. Now Seagoon, look into my eyes, toot toot toot . . . little daggers come out and point all the way along my eyes to his, toot toot toot . . . the secrets of Bottles mesmerism is bending Ned to my will . . . strainnnnn strainnnnn power of eyes, power of eyes . . . Ohhh squint, squint, squinteeee . . . Squin . . . ohh, my nose has started to bleed.
SEAGOON	You've crossed your eyes, you nit . . .
BLUEBOTTLE	Oh no! Den I'm finished with Russia, I am . . . I can't go out wid birds when my eyes are crossed.

SEAGOON	We've no time to lose.
BLUEBOTTLE	We must save Eccles from a death worse than fate.
SEAGOON	Yes, we must save Eccles.
BLOODNOK	Ah, but they never did . . . oh dear . . . to think you poor people came all this way just for that! Diddle diddle dum . . . well well, where are the pay-offs of yesteryear?
ORCHESTRA	**'OLD COMRADES MARCH' PLAYOUT**

THE SPY
OR WHO IS
PINK OBOE

The Goon Show, No. 252 (9th Series, No. 11)
Transmission:
Monday, 12th January 1959: 8.30—9.00 p.m. Home Service
Wednesday, 14th January 1959: 9.30—10.00 p.m. Light Programme
Studio: Paris Cinema, London

Written especially for Wagnerians (*1st July-31st June: Your month will be full of dramatic tension and harmony*), this episode recounts how the German spy Levingrin and the original designs of the Union Jack, the Union Jim, and the Union Dick, were tracked down by our coward Neddie Seagoon. His off-tune interpretation of 'La da die, dum die dum, lum da die dum' provides access to vital information concerning the disguise of the Berlin Philharmonic Orchestra as a Bavarian cabbage patch. Set in circa 1914, with inside leg 42, nostalgia reverberates throughout this enchanting story. Readers will recall bitterly such unashamed pleasures as Penelope, spam sandwiches, Bloodnok's dirigibles, and a set of priceless cuspidors. Sub-titles by Edie Ciano of Bromley.

The main characters

Ned Seagoon	Harry Secombe
Grytpype-Thynne	Valentine Dyall
Moriarty	Spike Milligan
Colonel Jim	Jack Train
Lieutenant Hugh Jympton	Spike Milligan
Eccles	Spike Milligan
Commander Nark	Kenneth Connor
Mr O'Toole	Kenneth Connor
Mrs O'Toole	Graham Stark
Enchantress	Kenneth Connor
Mysterious Man	Kenneth Connor
Jim	Spike Milligan
Willium	Kenneth Connor

(Peter Sellers was indisposed for this broadcast)

The Ray Ellington Quartet
Max Geldray
Orchestra conducted by Wally Stott
Announcer: Wallace Greenslade
Script by Spike Milligan
Produced by John Browell

THE SPY OR WHO IS PINK OBOE

BILL   This is the BBC Light Programme.

GRAHAM   (*tragic actor*) Pray say your Fertuffs quietly folks, as here is a High Fidelity recording of John Snagge.

GRAMS   **JOHN SNAGGE: This is the Satyricon of Petronius service of the Ba Be Sea, we apologise for the audience who attended the Goon Show on Sunday 28th December. It has been discovered that these people had actually written in for tickets to see a broadcast of Swedish drill by the Luton Girls Male choir, the actual Goon Show audience were misdirected to a gramophone recital of Jackson Pollock Paintings on clubbed leather. We apologise to all concerned. I will now kill myself.**

F.X.   **PISTOL SHOT. GROAN. THUD OF BODY.**

BILL   (*breaks down*) Ohh Master Snagge!

SEAGOON   Don't cry Walm he remembered you in his will.

BILL   How much???????

SEAGOON   Oh, no money, he just said, 'I remember Wal Greenslade'.

SPIKE   (*Indian*) Pardon me sir, but the Goon Show has broken out.

SEAGOON   Singes! We must volunteer for it at once. Forward!

GRAMS   **BRISK ARMY OF BOOTS MARCHING AWAY WITH HARRY SINGING: 'GIVE ME STOUT HEARTED MEN'.**

BILL   (*as song fades*) I too will volunteer for the Goon Show by announcing this announcement. We present, The Spy or —

GRAMS   **BILL (FAST) The Spy orrrrrrrrr (repeat).**

ORCHESTRA   **DRAMATIC CHORDS**

BILL   Meantime, in a deserted lock-keeper's lock the remains of French Aristocracy is steaming.

GRAMS   **FADE IN BOILING POT**

MORIARTY   (*sings*) Shine through my silent thoughts again . . . .

GRYTPYPE-THYNNE   I say, that smells good Moriarty, what is it?

MORIARTY   Me, I'm using Perfume de Sewers Devine on my knees.

GRYTPYPE-THYNNE   You erotic fool! You know full well that knee perfumes were the cause of Louis Cans downfall.

MORIARTY	Sapristi Doodle, Caramba le Ponk. You insult the knees of mon King mon Royalle de France. I challenge you to a seething duel. Name your weapon!
GRYTPYPE-THYNNE	I name my weapon Bazil. Now you name yours.
MORIARTY	I choose the Miserae at ten paces . . . .
HARRY	(*Announcer*) My Lords, ladies and gentlemen, this is a ten round . . . .
F.X.	**JELLY SPLOSH**

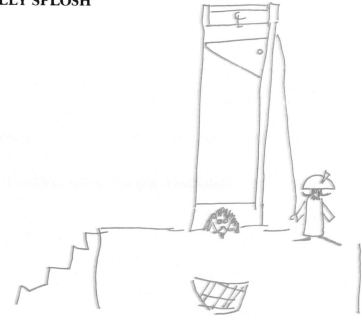

GRYTPYPE-THYNNE	Right in the old Dinner Disposer . . . .
MORIARTY	Now then, back to back. Ten paces and Sing . . . .
ORCHESTRA	**TIMID BELL SOFTLY THROUGH DUEL**
GRYTPYPE-THYNNE	(*sings*) In yon gloomy toerr. (*this duel grows in fury and determination as the singing continues*).
MORIARTY	(*off*) Miserae!
GRYTPYPE-THYNNE	Where death now is gleaming.
MORIARTY	Miserae!
GRYT-THYNNE	In death we shall meet no more.
MORIARTY	Miserae!
GRYTPYPE-THYNNE	On a cold winter's day.
MORIARTY	Miserae, Miserae MISERAEEEEEEEE (*goes mad*).
GRYTPYPE-THYNNE	And now to the HUH.
GRAMS	**DOUBLE FORTE JELLY SPLOSH**
MORIARTY	(*power*) You swine, you try to hit me with that unsigned sock full of grit. I'll not give in. Anything you can do I can do better.

GRAMS	**THE FOLLOWING RECORDED, GETTING FASTER AND FASTER**
GRYTPYPE-THYNNE	No you can't!
MORIARTY	Yes I can!
GRYTPYPE-THYNNE	No you can't!
MORIARTY	Yes I can!

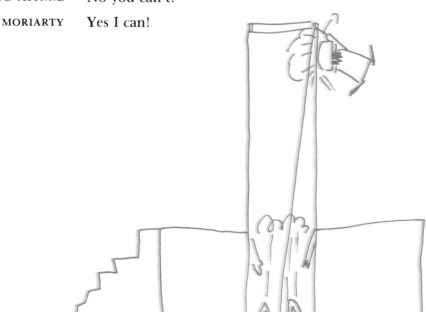

GRYTPYPE-THYNNE	No you can't!
MORIARTY	Yes I can!
GRYTPYPE-THYNNE	No you can't, no you can't, no you can't! . . . .
	(*pause*)
MORIARTY	Yes I cannnnnnnnnnnnnnn! . . . .
F.X.	**SLAPSTICK**
MORIARTY	Owwww!!!!! . . . .
GRAMS	**SPLASH — NORMAL SPEED**
MORIARTY	Help, I can't swim in water!
SEAGOON	Here, grab this copy of Bulganin's confession.
MORIARTY	Will it save me.
SEAGOON	It saved him. Now slide this piece of dry land under you.
GRAMS	**SOUND OF PUSHING A GRAND PIANO ON CASTORS OVER A WOODEN FLOOR. THE CASTORS BEING A BIT SQUEAKY TO GIVE THE SOUND OF TRACTION**
MORIARTY	Tarrrr.

GRYTPYPE-THYNNE	Yes, now Ned, for saving the Steam Count we charge a fee of three-shillings.
F.X.	**TILL**
GRYTPYPE-THYNNE	Thank you.
SEAGOON	Could you play that again?
F.X.	**TILL**
SEAGOON	What a lovely tune.
GRYTPYPE-THYNNE	Like it? It's the National Anthem of America. All the shops are playing it. Good Heavens! Then it's time for World War One . . . . on your marks.
F.X.	**PISTOL SHOT**
GRAMS	**GREAT RUSH AWAY OF MANY BOOTS, WITH A MILITANT BUGLE CALL OVER THE TOP**
MAX	That only leaves old Max 'Conks' Geldray.
MAX & ORCHESTRA	**MUSIC**

(*applause*)

BILL	Meantime in Whitehall . . . . plee pli plippy plee plo . . . .
JYMPTON	Excuse me Colonel Jim, sir, but er . . . . Captain Seagoon's bed has just pulled up outside, sir.
COLONEL JIM	Oh, he must be a late-riser, just a minute.
F.X.	**POP-POURING**
COLONEL JIM	I don't mind if I do. Come in Seagoon!
SEAGOON	(*approaching*) Hello, Colonel Jim, Sir.
Colonel Jim	How d'you do. Sit down my dear fellow, let me take some of your surplus legs from under your surplus.
SEAGOON	Thank you, mind if I play a violin?

COLONEL JIM	As long as it's one of ours.
SEAGOON	Care for one?
COLONEL JIM	Er, well just this once.
GRAMS	**TWO VIOLINS TUNING UP IN A VERY AMATEURISH WAY**
COLONEL JIM	By Jove, delicious, now Seagoon, do you know we're at war with naughty Germany?
SEAGOON	Well, I heard shouting . . . .
COLONEL JIM	Lieutenant Jympton? Tell him all.
JYMPTON	We need you sir, for counter espionage, sir.
SEAGOON	Ha ha ha, I suppose it means certain death?
COLONEL JIM	And a pension. A perfect combination.
SEAGOON	Well, it's for the old country, ha ha, Seagoons have never flinched from death.
ORCHESTRA	**BRING IN A MUTED TRUMPET AT SUNSET EFFECT**

SEAGOON	I can see it all now, I'll fight till me ammunitions gone. I'll say to the other men; Lads, make your way back as best as you can, ... me? I'll stay on, I'll fight 'em barehanded until I'm overpowered, and then I'll swallow my secret code. They'll torture me, I won't speak . . . . it'll mean the firing squad, ha ha. So what?
	They'll say; Any last requests? I say yes, damn you, I want evening dress . . . . I'll take my time and put it on with my full miniatures . . . . blind fold they'll say . . . . ha ha ha ha ha, the rifles'll come up, the click of the cartridges rammed home, they're taking aim . . . . ha ha ha . . . . I'll be smiling, that . . . . that carefree daredevil smile, the officer will raise his sword . . . . the volley will ring out, and I'll slump smiling to the floor — dead!
COLONEL JIM	Well, Seagoon?
SEAGOON	(*bloody coward*) I don't want to gooooo!·

GRAMS	**WHOOSH**
F.X.	**DOOR SLAMS**
COLONEL JIM	I say stop him before he gets to the bus stop.
GRAMS	**WHOOSH**
	(*pause*).
F.X.	**DOOR OPENS**
	(*struggle*)
SEAGOON	(*over above*) Let me go, I'm a professional coward I tell you . . . . I don't want to go to war.
JYMPTON	I caught him in Glasgow sir, wearing a Jewish kilt sir.
COLONEL JIM	My old regiment. Look Seagoon, there's a thousand pounds in it! If you succeed in this mission it will shorten the war by three-feet six-inches.
SEAGOON	So wars are being worn shorter this year?
COLONEL JIM	Of course.
SEAGOON	What's the job?
COLONEL JIM	Well a certain German spy has got the complete plans and measurements of the Union Jack. It's our job to stop him before he builds a prototype.
SEAGOON	Will they stop at nothing! Who is this fiend incarnate.
COLONEL JIM	Jympton, tell him.
JYMPTON	Have you ever heard of a German spy called (*sings*) 'la da die, dum die dum, lum da die dum' (*to tune march Lohengrin*). Have you heard of him?
SEAGOON	How do you spell it?
GRAMS	**SPIKE: SERIES OF STRANGE SOUNDS PLAYED AT SPEED**
SEAGOON	I think I'd recognise him if I heard him.
COLONEL JIM	Jolly good.
SEAGOON	Right. I'm your man.
ORCHESTRA	**DRAMATIC CHORDS**
BILL	A month has passed and we are now lumbered with a meeting of high military Freds.
HARRY	Gentlemen, tomorrow we start our great mission to recover those plans of the Union Jack. I have chosen you all for your intelligence.
ECCLES	You sure of dat?
HARRY	(*coughs*) There may be some slip-ups. Tomorrow we leave for France.

	Now this is the secret password: 'The wind is blowing through my grandmother's knees'. The reply is: 'Annie is waiting upstairs.'
ECCLES	Ohh, ho ho ho!
HARRY	I can see we're going to have trouble with you.
F.X.	**SLAPSTICK**
ORCHESTRA	**DRAMATIC CHORDS**
GRAMS	**LIGHT WIND, AND SEMI-DISTANT SOUND OF AIRSHIP ENGINES REVVING**
BILL	Dawn at Hendon Aerodrome, a freshly wallpapered airship is . . .
GRAMS	**ENGINE TICKING OVER . . . APPROACH OF JEEP. PULLS UP WITH SQUEAL OF BRAKES.**
BILL	. . . being shaved for active service.
SEAGOON	Morning Commander.
COMMANDER NARK	Good morning, now Seagoon these are the code-names. (You know I don't feel strange in this programme at all.) Do you know the code-names of our agents in France at all?
SEAGOON	(confidence) Carry on, I'll remember them.
COMMANDER NARK	There's the Black Rabbit, the Blue Pelican and the Yellow Alligator.
SEAGOON	(confidence) Roger.
COMMANDER NARK	Then there's the Octaroon Monkey, the Pink Oboe, and the Purple Mosquitoe.
SEAGOON	(getting worried) Yes, I think I . . .
COMMANDER NARK	Then there's the Vermillion Sock, the Vermillion Ponk, the Chocolate Speedway and the White Bint.
SEAGOON	Look, I . . . I think I'd better write this down.
COMMANDER NARK	No, you'll go colour blind . . .
GRAHAM	Excuse me sir, . . . Your airship's ready sir.
SEAGOON	Let me taste . . . (tastes) . . . Delicious . . . Right, tell Eccles to get inside, . . . Run my bath and lay out a Blonde Manequin.
GRAHAM	Hooray for war . . . ha ha (goes off).
VAL	I think we're going to have trouble with him too, Sir,
SEAGOON	Well, Goodbye fellas, and Hugh?
JYMPTON	Ah yes sir?
ORCHESTRA	**SAXOPHONE 'LAURA' A LA FILM BACKGROUND MUSIC**
SEAGOON	Hugh, say goodbye to Penelope for me . . .
JYMPTON	Yes, Goodbye Penelope.

SEAGOON	Not yet, you fool. When you see her. Tell her . . . tell her . . .
JYMPTON	Yes?
SEAGOON	I don't think I have got anything to tell her.
JYMPTON	Ahh, I'll tell her that then sir.
SEAGOON	Gad, how we've loved, passionate, by heavens, she's a hot little number.
JYMPTON	So I found after I married her sir.
SEAGOON	Ha, Ha. Ahemm yes, well, fair shares for all . . . goodbye . . .
OMNES	**Goodbye Sir!**
GRAMS	**ROAR OF THE GREAT AIRSHIPS ENGINES UP. GRADUALLY THEY FADE INTO DISTANCE. THEN SILENCE.**
SEAGOON	Who let go the rope before I got in?
COLONEL JIM	I say Seagoon, that boy was doing his duty, we wanted you to miss that airship, that's to be a decoy.
SEAGOON	How do I get to France then?
COLONEL	By this secret Military cycle.
SEAGOON	Gad, the war's as good as won. So saying, I hailed a taxi and cycled to Folkestone, there I caught a steam packet across the Channel, and as I drove my velosipy up the gang-plank, I saw another tricycle of foreign design upon my tail.
SPIKE	Gerblongen, gerkeinen, ich hatte sich un Edgware Road viereinen einegenauge *(etc.)*.
SEAGOON	It's old Milligan doing his impression of a naughty German there!
GRAMS	**BURST OF A MACHINE GUN. ZOOMING OF PLANES IN COMBAT . . . OCCASIONAL MACHINE GUN FIRE.**
SEAGOON	By turning my tricycle in a tight turn, I was on his tail and let him have a burst of steam.
GRAMS	**STEAMMMMMMM**
SPIKE	Achhhhhhh gerswchweinen.
GRAMS	**HOWL OF DOOMED FIGHTER PLANE . . . FADE**
SEAGOON	Got him! And so folks I shot down my first German tricycle. Waiting to sail, Old Man River Ellington played a merry shanty, and I went for the BRANDYYYYYY.
GRAMS	**RUSHING AWAY OF DRINK CRAZED BOOTS, SCREAMS AND SHOUTS**
RAY ELLINGTON QUARTET	**MUSIC**
	(applause).

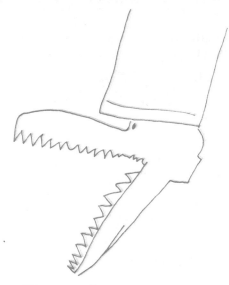

BILL	Part Three the spy. Pon tee tally tee.
ORCHESTRA	**SEA MUSIC**
GRAMS	**SEAGULLS OVER MUSIC. SHIPS TELEGRAPH. SOUND OF SEA.**
SEAGOON	Well, so far so good. I . . .
GRAMS	**BILL: (CAPTAIN) Hello all passengers, this is your Captain Merry Jim Greenslade speaking, here is a warning, this ship will be passing through fish infested waters, many of them sympathetic to the Germans, so therefore, there must be no naked lights on board.**
MR O'TOOLE	You hear that Mrs O'Toole? Put some clothes on that match.
MRS O'TOOLE	I'm looking for my Dorothy bag darlin'.
MR O'TOOLE	Oh, that old bag.
MRS O'TOOLE	But . . . I must find it, cocky.
MR O'TOOLE	Why, what's in it? What's in it Eh eh?
MRS O'TOOLE	You are . . . Darlin'.
MR O'TOOLE	Oh . . . Dear you naughty woman, you told me it was an overcoat sewn up at the bottom.
MRS O'TOOLE	We couldn't afford the fare Darlin'.
MR O'TOOLE	You got me into a Dorothy bag under false pretences . . . You darlin', darlin'.
BOTH	ARGUE. FADE.
ORCHESTRA	**VERY CORNY BUT WELL PLAYED SHORT LINK. ALL VERY NEAT BUT MEANS ABSOLUTELY NOTHING**

GRAMS	**AIRSHIP IN FLIGHT. THEN CHANGE TO AIRSHIP AS HEARD FROM INSIDE GONDOLA.**
BILL	We join the pilotless airship of the plotless story . . . with the luckless Eccles.
GRAMS	**BATH TAP RUNNING**
ECCLES	Ya de din tee nade de oi. Captain, your bath's ready . . . Captain? . . . Captain? . . . Captain? . . . Funny . . . I better go and see . . .
F.X.	**DOOR OPENS**
ECCLES	Oh! Pardon me Miss, have you seen Captain Seagoon?
ENCHANTRESS	No, I haven't darling.
ECCLES	Ohhhh, Yupahhhaho . . .
ENCHANTRESS	Tell me, tell me. What's your name?
ECCLES	My name is Eccles. Nooo . . . Rock Hudson . . . dats what I am, I'm Rock Hudson . . .
ENCHANTRESS	Well you come and sit down here Rocky, you naughty, naughty boy.
ECCLES	Oh her her he her hre hre reher . . .
F.X.	**KNOCKING ON DOOR**
ECCLES	Oh, ders somebody knocking at the airship door. At twenty-thousand feet?
ENCHANTRESS	He must be very tall.
ECCLES	I'm coming! Who's that out der.
F.X.	**DOOR OPENS. RUSH OF WIND OUTSIDE AIRSHIP.**
GRAHAM	I say, I say do help me, Eccles . . . I'm balancin' on a ladder and I'm being chased by a police ladder.
ECCLES	STRAINS . . . Ohhhhh.
F.X.	**DOOR SLAMS**
GRAHAM	I say Eccles, you do look rather weak and tired. Don't you think you sort of better get at the steering wheel. I say there's no-one steering, but that's silly. Ha ha ha ha ha ha.
ECCLES	I'd better watch this one.
GRAHAM	By Jove, fighting for England, if only my mother could see me now.
F.X.	**FAST PHONE RINGS UP QUICK**
GRAHAM	Hello is that you mother?
HARRY	*(German)* Is zat airship R.U.1.2?
GRAHAM	Yes, R.U.1.2.
HARRY	*(German)* Tell your pilot to put his hands, legs and teeth up, or I'll fire gerbang.

GRAHAM	Oh, do you know him then?
HARRY	(*German*) Dis is Von (*sings*) 'la da die, dum die dum, lum da die dum' (*Lohengrin*) .... I'm on your tail in a German fighter Triplane.
GRAHAM	Well, I tell you, he's awfully busy . . . can I tell him to ring you back later — say about three?
HARRY	Nein.
GRAHAM	Alright nine then.
HARRY	(*furious German*).
ECCLES	Give me dat here. Listen nutty I can't drive this airship wid my hands-up.
GRAMS	**BURST OF MACHINE GUN FIRE, ABOUT FIVE MACHINE GUNS AT DIFFERENT SPEEDS ALL OVER IN A BLASTING FLASH**
ECCLES	Ah . . . ahha . . . I'm learning though . . .
ORCHESTRA	**DRAMATIC CHORDS**
SEAGOON	When the ship docked in Paris, I was contacted by a mysterious man.
MYSTERIOUS MAN	Pssst . . . Pssst . . .
SEAGOON	He's got a puncture.
MYSTERIOUS MAN	Follow me while I'll follow you.
GRAMS	**RUNNING ALONG. TWO PAIRS OF BOOTS. PASS INTO DISTANCE.**
SEAGOON	For an hour we ran in French which I ran fluently. At Midnight we arrived at an old Chateau in Ville de Fon the foon.
JIM	Hello Jim 'The Wind is blowing through my Grandmother's knees' . . .
SEAGOON	'Annie is waiting upstairs'.
JIM	Good, menennnnn . . . he is one of us.
GRAHAM	Good, Thank heavens, he's not one of them dear.
JIM	Silence Madam X . . .
SEAGOON	Can you tell me anything about (*sings*) 'la da die, dum die dum, lum da die dum' (*Lohengrin*).
JIM	I know his whereabouts.
SEAGOON	Introduce me to them.
JIM	Very difficult Jim . . . very difficuuuuuullttt. Go to the Lonely Cross Roads at Rue de Postcards, there you will stand on one leg and whistle!
SEAGOON	Gad, I'll be whistling for England.
KEN	(*French*) 'ere Monsieur. First you must swallow zis alarm clock.

GRAMS	**MIX IN TICKING BEHIND DIALOGUE**
SEAGOON	*(gulps, mouth noises. Talks over the gulps).*
KEN	When it rings you'll know where it is at the time.
SEAGOON	Brilliant, farewell!
KEN	C'est un *Charlie.*
ORCHESTRA	**DRAMATIC CHORDS. WITH GERMAN HIGH COMMAND ATMOSPHERE.**
HARRY	*(German)* For zer last time tell me vere is British Agent, called *(sings)* 'Knees up Mudder Brune' is hiding.
ECCLES	Weee don't knoww, where Knees up Mudder Brown is hiding *(nonsense).*
HARRY	A likely story — here Davidson, tie zese men to a band of explosive saxophones.
ORCHESTRA	**DRAMATIC CHORDS.**
GRAMS	**LIGHT WIND, APPROACH OF NEDDIE RUNNING. STOPS IN FOREGROUND.**
SEAGOON	Ah these are the cross-roads, now stand on one leg and whistle. *(whistles very twittery Lohengrin).*
GRAMS	**JELLY SPLOSH IN FACE**
SEAGOON	Ohh err . . . spuk . . . err . . . Who threw that enemy Christmas pudding?
GRYTPYPE-THYNNE	Quick, tie his teeth behind his back, before he can eat it.
SEAGOON	You devils, you'll hear from my solicitor about this . . .
GRAMS	**LOUD TICKING**
MORIARTY	There's something ticking inside his stomach!
GRYTPYPE-THYNNE	It must be a stomach bomb, run for it!
GRAMS	**FURIOUS RUNNING AND SCREAMING BY THYNNE & MORIARTY**
WILLIUM	'Ere, was that you whistling on one leg, mate?
SEAGOON	Yes. *(slowly)* 'The wind is whistling up my grandmother's knees'.
WILLIUM	Oh, she orter wear long draws then, mate! ha ha!
SEAGOON	That was a secret code you nit. He wasn't at rehearsal you know.
WILLIUM	I'm not with it yet.
SEAGOON	I don't think we are either.
WILLIUM	I've an important word mate, 'Annie is waiting upstairs'.
SEAGOON	Good. Who are you?
WILLIUM	I'm Pink Oboe.

SEAGOON	Good heavens, Ted Ray's grandfather.
WILLIUM	And I can prove it. Now listen, Eccles is in danger.
SEAGOON	This is going to be a happy ending folks!
WILLIUM	Now get that wheel-barrow there and foller me.
GRAMS	**TRUNDLING A WHEELBARROW ALONG. ONE MAN'S BOOTS RUNNING EFFECT AS IF A MAN RUNNING AND PUSHING THE BARROW.**
ORCHESTRA	**BRIEF DRAMATIC CHORDS**
GRAMS	**CHAINS STRUGGLES**
BILL	*(over)* In here agent 'knees up Mother Brown' . . .
SEAGOON	*(coming out of the music)* Let me go, you German devils you.
F.X.	**IRON PRISON DOOR SLAMS**
SEAGOON	Swines. *(sniff)* Funny smell in here — Bloodnok!
ECCLES	He's not in, it's me 'over in the corner, I'm tied to an exploding saxophone. Quick!
SEAGOON	Let me —
GRAMS	**EXPLOSION**
F.X.	**CLOCK FALLS ON FLOOR TICKING**
ECCLES	Oh — Neddie? Well, that's the sad story of Agent Ned . . . all that's left . . .
GRAMS	**BRING IN ALARM CLOCK TICKING**
ECCLES	. . . is this clock he swallowed.
GRAMS	**ALARM GOES**
ECCLES	Oh dear, time for beddy-byes. Where's my dolly?
ENCHANTRESS	Here I am darling.
ECCLES	I'm not that young fellas . . .
ORCHESTRA	**'OLD COMRADES MARCH' PLAYOUT**

CALL OF THE WEST

The Goon Show, No. 254 (9th Series, No. 12)
Transmission:
Tuesday, 20th January 1959: 8.30—9.00 p.m. Home Service
Wednesday, 21st January 1959: 9.30—10.00 p.m. Light Programme
Studio: Camden Theatre, London

THRILL to the noble atrocities of illiterate Captain Slokum and
the 9th U.S. Cavalry!

SIGH to the romantic strains of Tex Maclength and his sons
of the bicycle-saddle!

STRAIN to the unrestrained rhythms of Bloodnok's thunderpills!

Yes, here, for the first time on the wide-screen of the wireless, the
true story of how the wild-west was won. Set in East Finchley, the
drama recounts how the Indian tribes cut off supplies from Fort
Fertanggg with just 29 explosive saxophones and a crate of fish
bones. Hindered by the insanitary exploits of 'Mad Dan' Eccles
aboard the No. 49 bus, Bluebottle massacres the entire tribe
single-handed with his cardboard cut-out pistol.

Note: Miss Miriam Reene of 33 Croft Street, East Finchley, has
been left out of this script in order to protect a man called Tom
Mountain.

The main characters

Ned Seagoon	Harry Secombe
Little Jim	Spike Milligan
American Bum	Peter Sellers
Grytpype-Thynne	Peter Sellers
Moriarty	Spike Milligan
'Davey' Eccles	Spike Milligan
Captain Slokum	Peter Sellers
Lootenant Hern-Hern	Harry Secombe
Sergeant Fladoo	Spike Milligan
Dr Denis Bloodnok	Peter Sellers
Coolie	Spike Milligan
Bluebottle	Peter Sellers
Bluebottle's mum	Harry Secombe
Henry Crun	Peter Sellers
Minnie Bannister	Spike Milligan
Old Uncle Oscar	Harry Secombe

The Ray Ellington Quartet
Max Geldray
Orchestra conducted by Wally Stott
Announcer: Wallace Greenslade
Script by Spike Milligan
Produced by John Browell

CALL OF THE WEST

BILL	This is the BBC.
HARRY	Good. Now Walm here is that same announcement by a midget.
GRAMS	**HARRY: This is the BBC Home Service. (FAST)**
BILL	Who's he?
HARRY	I'm a friend of Bert Fertanggggg!
PETER	Fertannnggggg?
HARRY	Fertunggggg.
PETER	Sfhnitouuuuuuu.
HARRY	Toweeeeeeeeee.
	(*repeat from Fertanggggggg, with variations*)
GRAMS	**CARRY ON THE ABOVE SOUNDS AT A HIGHER SPEED**
BILL	Dear Spontellibons, you are listening to the sound track of this week's wonder ear film, presenting! Captain Stingo! or . . . .
PETER	Goon Law, or, or anythingggggggg. Hern . . . .
ORCHESTRA	**WESTERN GUN LAW THEME**
F.X.	**ELECTRONIC GUN WITH ABOVE**
ORCHESTRA	**TAKE THE THEME UNDER THE NARRATION AND KEEP IT GOING ppp WITH A SORT OF AMERICAN FRONTIER MARCH . . . . VERY ppp.**
PETER	(*over music*) See, hear and smell hairless-midget Harry Seagoon as Double Captain Rapture, hard-riding, hard-shooting, hard-up cowboy.
SEAGOON	(Kensington accent) Hello you 'orny critters.
PETER	This role calls for great audience imagination. See, feel and hit, Spike Milligna as the dying actor.
F.X.	**PISTOL SHOT.**
SPIKE	Owwwwwwwwwwww!

HARRY	Yes for the first time on your radio screen, see the hand operated electric teeth of Peter 'Voices' Sellers and Big Black Beauty, the Mad Wallpapered Stallion.
GRAMS	**GALLOPING BOOTS. THIS CAN BE DONE BY SOMEONE OPERATING A PAIR OF BOOTS IN THE SAME METER AS COCONUT SHELLS. OVERLAP WITH THE MULE. ALL SPEED-UP.**
HARRY	Listen to the strains of Tex MacLength and his sons of the bicycle saddle.
GRAMS	**GOONS: ALL SING 'GIVE ME A HOME'. FASTER THAN NORMAL. ALL LAID OUT BY THE SOUND OF THREE TUBULAR BELLS BELTING THEM ON THE HEAD. ALL FADE OFF GROANING. 'Oh me nut' etc.**
BILL	This then, is your entertainment for this evening.
GRAMS	**THE WHOLE AUDIENCE SCREAM AND RUN FOR THE EXITS.**
ORCHESTRA	**RESTATE NEW NOBLE WESTERN THEME. FADE UNDER.**
GRAMS	**WHARFSIDE SOUNDS**
BILL	It is 1867, and dead on time, the harbour of Boston is a hive of inactivity, as English immigrants bring their shattered bank accounts to the New World. Alongside is the good ship Venus. The Pling-plang toof noppity nippity noo, plita. Omnivirous, plethora. Platty plong plong ta te ti to tue . . . fnit, poll. Tong, tang ting, putt putt . . . I say, I can't read this rubbish I . . . Ooo!
GRAMS	**SPLASH**
LITTLE JIM	He's fallen in the water.
SEAGOON	Yes sonny, it's a tradition among drowning men . . . Come let's step ashore onto America, the land of plenty.
AMERICAN BUM	Bud, you got a nickle for a cupa coffee?
SEAGOON	You poor man, you must be starving, here, take that.
GRAMS	**ELECTRONIC BASH IN THE FACE. ADD JELLY SPLOSH.**
AMERICAN BUM	Owwwww, buddy.
SEAGOON	That'll teach him not to be poor in front of me again. Fill the horses up with three-gallons of hay. Ha ha ha what a gallant figure I must have made, in my tricorned hat, tricorned trousers and an unexpurgated first edition of the Union Jack.
GRYTPYPE-THYNNE	Did you say covered wagon? Look here, I too am heading west with this retired wooden fish-crate.
MORIARTY	*(muffled)* Owww. Let me out of here, Grytpype . . . the fumes, Oh the fumes . . . Oh the pong they make.
SEAGOON	I say. What are those yellow things champing at the knothole?

GRYTPYPE-THYNNE	They are the teeth of a dear friend and confidante, the great French poet and lyric plumber, Count Jim 'Flies' . . .
GRAMS	**GREAT BUZZING OF FLIES UP AND OUT**
GRYTPYPE-THYNNE	. . . Moriarty.
SEAGOON	Oh, why does he travel by fish-crate?
GRYTPYPE-THYNNE	It's something to do with the devaluation of the Franc, I'm not sure. However, apart from which he is inventing something.
GRAMS	**ALTO SAX: PLAYS 'SAX O PHUN' (AS HEARD FROM INSIDE A CRATE. PLAYED BACK FASTER)**
GRYTPYPE-THYNNE	E'en now he treads the keys of his adult saxophone, my dear sir. Listen? . . . . He's working on it. Could we hire perchance a room on your covered-wagon so that the Count may continue undisturbed, by disturb?
SEAGOON	Well, there's no bath.
GRYTPYPE-THYNNE	No bath? Just what the Count likes at the end of a long day.
SEAGOON	Right, now where's the rent?
GRYTPYPE-THYNNE	In my trousers.
SEAGOON	He bent down, and sure enough . . . He had a rent in his trousers.
ORCHESTRA	**TA RA CHORD**
SEAGOON	(sings) California! Here we come . . . GID UP THERE!
GRAMS	**WAGON WHIPS CRACKING. WAGONS MOVING OFF ETC.**
ORCHESTRA	**WESTERN PLAINS MUSIC. 'I COME FROM ALABAMA WITH A BANJO ON MY KNEE' . . . WITH MOUTH ORGAN LEAD. (INTO MAX GELDRAY'S NUMBER)**
MAX & ORCHESTRA	**MUSIC**
	(Applause)
GRAMS	**NIGHT. DISTANT CRICKETS. DISTANT HOWL OF A PRAIRIE DOG.**
SEAGOON	I say, will those prairie dogs never stop howling?
GRYTPYPE-THYNNE	They're always howling, no trees on prairie.
SEAGOON	Listeners who recognise that gag please keep their traps shut . . . Well, I'm going to bed . . . Goodnight.
GRAMS	**GREAT SQUEAKING AND COMPRESSING OF BED SPRINGS. BREAKING, CREAKING, ETC.**
SEAGOON	Eighteen-stone three, gad I'm a heavy sleeper.
MORIARTY	(muffled) Let me outtt . . .
GRYTPYPE-THYNNE	Shh, quiet in that crate.

MORIARTY	It is night or day?
GRYTPYPE-THYNNE	Fool . . . that sort of thing is only for the rich.
MORIARTY	Let me out.
GRYTPYPE-THYNNE	I'll let you out, when you've made enough saxophones to sell to the Indians.
MORIARTY	I've made 500. *(raves)*
F.X.	**CHAINS AND DOOR OPENING**
GRYTPYPE-THYNNE	Have you? Well come out. Now which of all these fish-bones is you.
MORIARTY	I'm the one with hairs on.
GRAMS	**DISTANT WAR WHOOPS MIXED WITH CHICKENS CLUCKING**
SEAGOON	*(over above)* The Indians are attacking on the new wide screen!
GRAMS	**WAR WHOOPS — SHOOTING. THUNDER OF INDIAN HORSES CIRCLING THE WAGONS. SHOOTING IN DIFFERENT PERSPECTIVES.**
ECCLES	*(sings)* Born on a mountain top in Tennessee born in . . . *(mumble)*
SEAGOON	What luck, it's Davey Eccles in his goon-shin cat.
ECCLES	Want luck itls Calven Cleccet nil in Glone sklint atamt . . . *(gurgles)*
SEAGOON	Do it good and you can clean it up later . . . Now, listen, we need help, those Indians are overpowering us.
SEAGOON	Get through to Fort Fertangg, and fetch help, here's the fare.
ECCLES	Taaaaa gid-up.
GRAMS	**OMNIBUS DRIVES AWAY**
SEAGOON	Fortunately for us folks, a bare ten-miles away the U.S. 9th Cavalry were in the area and . . . a bare ten miles in America is equal to three fully-clothed-miles in France ha ha ahem.
GRAMS	**THUNDER OF TROOP OF CAVALRY AT GALLOP**
CAPTAIN SLOKUM	Woahh.
GRAMS	**HORSES STOP DEAD**
CAPTAIN SLOKUM	That's descipline for yer. *(spit)*
F.X.	**DANG**
CAPTAIN SLOKUM	Lootenant Hern-Hern?
GRAMS	**MAN RUNS FROM THE BACK OF THE COLUMN VERY BRISKLY**
Lt. HERN-HERN	*(breathless)* Yes Sir?
CAPTAIN SLOKUM	Where's yer hoss?

Lt. HERN-HERN	You only called me, Sir.
CAPTAIN SLOKUM	That's a good answer son, you must be mighty proud of it.
Lt. HERN-HERN	It belonged to my father Hern.
CAPTAIN SLOKUM	It's a well worn Hern . . . here's a dollar Hern
Lt. HERN-HERN	A dollar Hern . . . what for Hern?
CAPTAIN SLOKUM	It's a pay as you Hern. *(spit)*
F.X.	**DANG**
CAPTAIN SLOKUM	Sergeant Fladoo? Where's the Chuck Wagon Hern?
Sgt. FLADOO	Heren heren heren *(rubbish)*
CAPTAIN SLOKUM	If you say so. *(spit)*
GRAMS	**JELLY SPLOSH IN FACE**
CAPTAIN SLOKUM	I'm sorry Sarge, here catch this life-belt.
GRAMS	**SPLASH**
Lt. HERN-HERN	We better get going Colonel, they say that Nobblynee red-Indians are in the vicinity.
BILL MAX RAY	*(off sing)* I'll be calling youuuuuuuuuu oooooooo ooooooooooo.
BILL	*(sing)* And I'll answer . . .
TRIO	*(sing)* Toooooo . . . oooooo . . . oooooo . . .
Lt. HERN-HERN	It's three lone Indians.

CAPTAIN SLOKUM	Call'em over we could do with a loan Hern.
Lt. HERN-HERN	Great jumping Fernakerpans, it's the Nobblynee tribe and in full war-paint and wall-paper.
RAY	Ughhhhhhh. How. Ugggg. Ugh ta.
CAPTAIN SLOKUM	I reckon there must be an easier way to make a living you know. How . . . Hern . . . How.
RAY	Me Chief Investor in Wall Street . . . Chief Sitting Bull and Bear, this my squaw.
BILL	How do you do?
RAY	Uggggggggg!
CAPTAIN SLOKUM	Yes, I thought that, too.
RAY	And this nit here is my son, great warrior, Fred Smith OBE.
MAX	Hello boy, I had eggs for tea.
CAPTAIN SLOKUM	Eh? He looks mighty tall in the saddle.
RAY	That's because it's on a horse, mate.
BILL MAX RAY	TA RAAAAAAAA!
CAPTAIN SLOKUM	Chief, we want to do business. We're willin' to knock all your teeth out for nothin' and give you genuine false ones in exchange for your old buffalo hides.
RAY	Mmmmm. Ugggg, all my braves have buffalo hides.
CAPTAIN SLOKUM	Well, where's yours?
RAY	Where's my what mate?
CAPTAIN SLOKUM	Where's your buffalo hide?
RAY	He's hiding behind that tree mate.
BILL MAX RAY	TA RAAAAAAAAA!

80

RAY Me no like what white man offer, you go, or my braves go on four-lane warpath ... now give you biff on conk. Biff!

PETER *(small voice)* That's my dad boy!

CAPTAIN SLOKUM Watch out Sittin' Bull. I'll get you as sure as my name's Custer ...

F.X. **(OFF) COCONUT SHELLS**

ECCLES *(off)* Oh here here here.

Lt. HERN-HERN Smoke, it's something going here here here.

ECCLES It was me going here ... here, here, here.

CAPTAIN SLOKUM Steady there son.

ECCLES The Wagon Train wid your wife on board is being attacked by the Injuns.

CAPTAIN SLOKUM Ma Wife? Is she safe?

ECCLES Yer.

CAPTAIN SLOKUM I never did like them Injuns.

Lt. HERN-HERN Did any follow you?

ECCLES Yer, they were shooting all the time. But I just stuck my tongue out at 'em.

Lt. HERN-HERN Get wounded?

ECCLES Yer.

Lt. HERN-HERN Where?

ECCLES In the tongue.

Lt. HERN-HERN For no reason at all — forward! ...

GRAMS **TROOP OF CAVALRY GALLOP OFF: CHORUS: SING 'TEXAS RANGER SONG' FROM RIO RITA. ALL AT SPEED. FADE.**

BILL That night the tribes were assembled for War. A white man and his fish-crate were the centre of attraction.

GRYTPYPE-THYNNE	I come as a fellow Equity member, with all dues paid. First I knock on box so . . .
F.X.	**WALLOP**
MUSIC	**TENOR SAX: 'TOITS DE PAREE'**
ORCHESTRA & OMNES	**RED INDIAN AMAZEMENT SOUNDS**
GRYTPYPE-THYNNE	Yes, we bring you saxophones.
BOTH	'From out of the sky, my brother and IIIIIIIII . . .'
HARRY	Ugh, me like, me try play.
MUSIC	**DESPERATE ATTEMPT TO PLAY 'RAMONA' OR 'THE INDIAN LOVE CALL'**
MORIARTY	You play lovely chief, lovely.
GRYTPYPE-THYNNE	Yes, he plays lovely, doesn't he? It could easily pass for music. And I'd pass it.
HARRY	Good, tonight me and braves attack white man with Saxophone ughhhhh . . . Minnie ha ha hahahahahaha.
GRAMS	**SOUNDS OF DOZENS OF ALTO SAXOPHONES BEING PLAYED. TOM TOMS. AND WAR WHOOPS. FADE OUT, FADE IN.**
CAPTAIN SLOKUM	Gentlemen, somebody's supplying the Indians with saxophones. *(spit)*
SEAGOON	I think I know . . . who did it.
F.X.	**DANG**
CAPTAIN SLOKUM	Bring that thing closer will you? You were saying Hern?
SEAGOON	I know who they are . . . Moriarty and Thynne.
CAPTAIN SLOKUM	Where's they hiding?
SEAGOON	America.
CAPTAIN SLOKUM	Sergeant, make a note of that address.
Sgt. FLADOO	How do you spell it?
CAPTAIN SLOKUM	Don't bother how to spell it, just write it down.
F.X.	**FURIOUS WRITING**
CAPTAIN SLOKUM	Now read it back.
Sgt. FLADOO	Mra aggaraowowowowwwwww.
CAPTAIN SLOKUM	Yer, that sounds like the place. Right men, search America and look under the beds.
GRAMS	**TROOP OF CAVALRY GALLOP OFF. CHORUS SING: 'TEXAS RANGER' SONG FROM THE FILM RIO RITA. ALL SPEED UP.**

MORIARTY	Grytpype, they've got wind of us, we got to get away I tell you.
F.X.	**SLAPSTICK**
GRYTPYPE-THYNNE	Don't panic. Get into this women's disguise-kit while Ray Ellington releases his power of songs on an unsuspecting world.
RAY ELLINGTON QUARTET	**MUSIC.**
	(Applause)
BILL	Meantime in Dodge City, television centre of the old west, a Quack hawkes his wares, and wears his hawkes . . . whichever way is the better.
ORCHESTRA	**BLOODNOK THEME. WITH BOOMING BASS DRUM & HAND OPERATED CYMBALS (BLOODNOK SHOUTS 'ROLL UP').**
GRAMS	**BUBBLING CAULDRON THAT EXPLODES**
BLOODNOK	Oh that's done me a power of good folks. And there's more where that come from folks. Citizens of Dodge City. Bloodnok's the name. Dr Denis Bloodnok, late of Harley Street, Twickenham. I've cured the aristocrats of the Plinn the Farmers. Let me read this testimonial, 'Dear Sir, since taking your course of Thunder Pills, I feel like a new man, Signed, Mrs Ivy Chandler.' Now then who will be first to try it, I say.
ORCHESTRA	**MURMURS AMONG THE CROWD**
COOLIE	I'll try some of that, Sir.
BLOODNOK	A Hindu Rajah. Give him a big hand.
COOLIE	Thank you, Sir, but I am only a coolie.
BLOODNOK	Coolie? Give him a small hand.
GRAMS	**RECORDING OF SMALL APPLAUSE. (VERY SHORT)**
BLOODNOK	Now then mystic son of the East, sip this small sulphur and liquorice bomb . . .
COOLIE	*(mouth noises).*
BLOODNOK	Look! Before my eyes, before my military eyes . . .
GRAMS	**MAN EXPLODES: ELECTRONIC.**
COOLIE	Oh, good heavens, where are my trousers?
BLOODNOK	How do you feel Prince of the East?
COOLIE	I don't feel well, I feel very, very ill.

TO THE THEATRE →

BLOODNOK	Ill?
HARRY	You're a quack, mister.
BLOODNOK	Steady Yankee Doodles, or I'll have the Red Coats on you. I'm a personal friend of Billy Butlin you know.
ORCHESTRA	**THREATS OF HANG HIM: GROW IN SIZE: BLOODNOK PROTESTS.**
GRAMS	**BLOODNOK: Helpppppppp LONE PAIR OF BOOTS DEPARTING FOLLOWED BY THE THUNDER OF THE BOOTS OF A MOB. ELECTRONIC GUN SHOTS. VOCAL SOUND OF THE MOB CONTINUE BUT HELD UNDER JANGLE BOX PIANO: BAR ROOM SOUNDS.**
GRYTPYPE-THYNNE	I say, barman, drinks for my lady.
MORIARTY	I'll have a glass of Fish and Chips.
GRYTPYPE-THYNNE	And see you put a good head on it.
RAY	Man we don't keep any drink called fish and chips.
GRYTPYPE-THYNNE	What! Come Moriarty we'll take our trade and malnutrition elsewhere.
Lt. HERN-HERN	Hold everything! I'm Lootenant Hern-Hern of the United States Cavalry, reasonable charges to regular customers . . . Now we're looking for two men who've been selling contraband saxophones to the Red Injuns . . . thereby causing unemployment among white musicians.
MORIARTY	Ohahahahooooooo.
Lt. HERN-HERN	*(suspicious)* Pardon me Maam, your . . . a . . . your wig's fallen off.
GRYTPYPE-THYNNE	Wig? How dare you . . . the unfortunate woman just happens to have gone bald suddenly . . . it's obviously a case of the new lightning French alapecha . . . from the song of the same name.

MORIARTY	That's right *(sings to tune Aloetta)* 'Alapecha lightning alapecha... alapecha... happens everyday.'
GRYTPYPE-THYNNE	*(sings)* 'First you get it on your nut'...
MORIARTY	*(sings)* 'First you get it on your nut'...
F.X.	**THWACK**
MORIARTY	*(sings)* Ohh my nut...
GRYTPYPE-THYNNE	*(sings)* Oh his nut...
MORIARTY	*(sings)* Oh my nut.
ORCHESTRA	**OOOOOOOOOOOH... Alapecha lightning alapecha....**
Lt. HERN-HERN	Woww... stop that alapecha... One moment you two... I seem to recognise your face sir, take off that false nose... Ahha... now them false ears... now that false suit... now that false chest... just as I thought... I don't know who you are. Who are you?
GRYTPYPE-THYNNE	Lord Nelson.
Lt. HERN-HERN	He had one arm missin'.
GRYTPYPE-THYNNE	I have... I used to have three.
ECCLES	Hello Captain... care to join us for a hand of cards?
Lt. HERN-HERN	Poker, Pontoon or rummy?
ECCLES	Yer yer... and cards...
CAPTAIN SLOKUM	Alright fellas... I pass.
Lt. HERN-HERN	I pass.
ECCLES	Mmmmm... it's up to me now... I'm callin' you fellas.

BLUEBOTTLE	Oooh . . . he's calling us *all* fellas . . . It's the call of the West partner . . . chews plug of Hopalong Cassidy cardboard string tobacco . . . spit spit spitteee . . . ohh . . . it's gone right down the front of my shirt.
Lt. HERN-HERN	Who are you stranger? . . . speak up!
BLUEBOTTLE	I am . . . Marshall Matt Dillon . . . of 23 Flubb Avenue . . . East Finchley North 12.
Lt. HERN-HERN	I ain't never seen you in Dodge City before . . . how did you get here?
BLUEBOTTLE	I come on the 49 bus from the High Street.
Lt. HERN-HERN	There ain't no buses run out here.
BLUEBOTTLE	No it only took me as far as the Odeon then I had to walk the rest of the way myself.
ECCLES	What about the game?
Lt. HERN-HERN	O.K. then . . . . you're calling Mad Dan . . . . what kind of hand you got?
ECCLES	Four fingers and a thumb.
BLUEBOTTLE	I beat you mad Dan . . . . I got four fingers, two thumbs and a toe.
ECCLES	A toe? There ain't such a hand.
BLUEBOTTLE	Do you think I'm a cheat?
ECCLES	No, I think you're deformed.
BLUEBOTTLE	No man can call Bluebottle deformed unless he is a specialist . . . . Eccles I'm running you in.

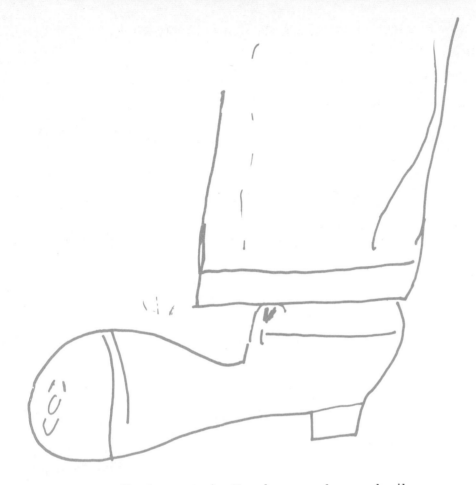

ECCLES	I've been run in, I've done ten-thousand miles.
Lt. HERN-HERN	Come on Mad Dan . . . . are you going quietly . . . . or do we have to use ear plugs?
BLUEBOTTLE	Go for your guns Mad Dan . . . . I'm warning you . . . . see the panther like movement of my mittened hands as they curl towards the cardboard and string triggers of my cut-out pistol . . .
F.X.	**DOOR OPENS**
BLUEBOTTLE'S MUM	There you are, you dirty little tramp . . . .
BLUEBOTTLE	Ooooh Mum . . . .
BLUEBOTTLE'S MUM	I'll give you oh mum . . . . your father's been looking everywhere for his trilby hat . . . . where's all the shopping I sent you for?
F.X.	**SLAPSTICKS**
BLUEBOTTLE	(*over above*) Oh mum . . . . you've spoilt my game . . . . ooh . . . . bye bye Eccles . . . .
F.X.	**DOOR SLAMS**
GRYTPYPE-THYNNE	And so perish all enemies of the Queen.
MORIARTY	And there's more where that came from.

Lt. HERN-HERN	Now I recognise that voice by the shape of those words.
GRYTPYPE-THYNNE	Run for it Moriarty.... they know us.
GRAMS	**TWO WHOOSHES**
ORCHESTRA	**SHORT SHARP DRAMATIC CHORDS**
BILL	This then was the situation. Bloodnok pursued by the mob, Grytpype pursued by the 9th Cavalry and Bluebottle pursued by his mother. With that in mind will listeners please take in their slack and listen to the occupants of Fort Fertang preparing for the Indian Assault.
F.X.	**LOADING BLUNDERBUSSES WITH CHAINS AND SMALL SHOT**
CRUN	Ahhh, they won't quell old Hen Crun by surprise.... Min stand against that wall for a certain test.
MINNIE	O.K. Cocky.
GRAMS	**BLUNDERBUSSES FULL OF RUBBISH DISCHARGED. MIN SCREAMS**
CRUN	Did that hurt, Min?
MINNIE	Yes....
CRUN	Good, then this is the gun for them.
MINNIE	I hope they attack soon, the dinner's getting burnt.
CRUN	They'll never attack a burnt dinner, Min.
OLD UNCLE OSCAR	(approaches) Owow mamamamamm.... aha.... ahhhhhhahah ahh.
CRUN	Oh, Uncle Oscar, what are you doing out of your grave?
MINNIE	He must be feeling better.
OLD UNCLE OSCAR	Ohhhahaha.... hahahahah.... ahahahah.... ahahah amamamamahahahaha.
CRUN	Oh Uncle at your age, you been at the hormones again....
OLD UNCLE OSCAR	Ahahahahah.... amamamam.... an ahaahanahabannnnnn
F.X.	**HANDFUL OF TEETH FALL ON FLOOR**
CRUN	There go his teeth Min.... that means more dinner for us.
GRAMS	**SERIES OF STRANGE INDIAN WAR WHOOPS (DISTANT)**
CRUN	Ohhhh hear that Min. It's the war-whoops of the Nakertacker Indian
MINNIE	Are they the ones that commit atrocities?
CRUN	Yes Min.
MINNIE	I'll go upstairs and get ready.
CRUN	Stop it do you hear Min, you know that's.... for meeeee....

OLD UNCLE OSCAR	Ahhhhhhhhhh hahhhhhhhhhh.
CRUN	He remembers Min. Now Uncle get inside that coffin and defend it with your life. Now, I'll just announce the next part of the programme. Ladies and gentlemen, I have pleasure in announcing a knock at the door.
F.X.	**DOOR BELL RINGS**
CRUN	Blast, there's been a change in the programme . . . . Who is it?
BILL	And so folks, we say goodnight from happydom.
GRAMS	**PISTOL SHOT**
BLOODNOK	Ah, he got me folks, another unhappy ending especially for me.
F.X.	**SPIT BUCKET AS PREVIOUS**
ORCHESTRA	**'I WANT TO BE HAPPY' PLAYOUT**

THE SCARLET CAPSULE

The Goon Show, No. 255 (9th Series, No. 14)
Transmission:
Monday, 2nd February 1959: 8.30—9.00 p.m. Home Service
Wednesday, 4th February 1959: 9.30—10.00 p.m. Light Programme
Studio: Paris Cinema, London

In 1903, the £22 fine that London Transport paid for assisting illegal immigrants caused immediate bankruptcy. Our story, set in the 21st Century, tells how a group of rusting archeologists discovered rotting commuter skulls near Finchley Central. Further digging reveals the mysterious grafitti-ridden scarlet capsule. Could this be the lost Kingdom of the Northern Line, or merely an out of order telephone box? Leading demon Ned Quartermess is brought in to investigate, and immediately things deteriorate. With his Jewish kilt at half-mast, our expert is baffled by the insignificance of Minnie's Irish stews.

The main characters

Willium	Peter Sellers
Murphy	Spike Milligan
Taffy	Harry Secombe
Henry Crun	Peter Sellers
Minnie Bannister	Spike Milligan
Ned Quartermess	Harry Secombe
Major Denis Bloodnok	Peter Sellers
Eccles	Spike Milligan
Bluebottle	Peter Sellers
Breathy Kensington Dear	Peter Sellers

The Ray Ellington Quartet
Max Geldray
Orchestra conducted by Wally Stott
Announcers: Wallace Greenslade & Andrew Timothy
Script by Spike Milligan
Produced by John Browell

THE SCARLET CAPSULE

BILL	This is the BBC.
PETER	Hold it up to the light — not a brain in sight.
HARRY	Ah John Friar Sellers, taste this script.
PETER	(*fast eating*) What is it?
HARRY	A freshly cooked version of —
ORCHESTRA	**SPINE TINGLING CHORDS**
	(*leading to*)
GRAMS	**QUATERMASS OSCILLIATION**
PETER	Quartermess OBE.
ORCHESTRA	**CONCLUDING CHORDS** (*fade*)
ANDREW TIMOTHY	This is the Terror stricken service of the BBC. Today, at approximately this afternoon, a discovery was made on the sight of the Notting Hill Gate site of the Government's new 'Dig up the Roads plan for congesting traffic Scheme'. Workmen, in the absence of a strike settled for work as an alternative. It was during this brief lull in high powered inertia that Maurice Onions, a scaffolders knee wrencher, stumbled across something he'd found. Tinggg . . . Tonggg . . . Billy Bonggg. I would like it known that though I read this stuff, I don't write it. Fertangggg!
GRAMS	**SOUNDS OF A ROAD BUILDERS GANG**
WILLIUM	Here, here Julian over here, mate here. Get yer trousers on — hurry Julian. Look at — this!
ORCHESTRA	**DRAMATIC CHORD**
GRAMS	**WITH ABOVE: QUATERMASS, COMIC OSCILLATIONS**
MURPHY	Oh dear, Saints preserve us.
TAFFY	Hey, what's this all about . . . . ohh, that's a human skull.
WILLIUM	Is it?
TAFFY	Ay, must be a woman . . . . the mouth's open. Ha ha.
MURPHY	We better call an Irish doctor.

TAFFY	Too late for that, she's a gooner for sure.
WILLIUM	Call the Chinese Police . . . . here hold this whistle and play that note.
F.X.	**POLICE WHISTLE. GIVE A HEFTY BLAST**
GRAMS	**ONE PAIR OF BOOTS APPROACH AT A COLLOSAL SPEED. SLOW-UP VERY QUICKLY TO A HALT.**
MURPHY	(*over above*) Listen he's coming, he's almost here, he's arrived.
BILL	(*breathless*) You were playing my song — I'm sorry I'm late but the flinn of the flonn sclunned the nib of the Ploon.
TAFFY	A likely story, now have a look at this.
BILL	Gad, the head of a skull. I'd better take its finger prints. Ladies and gentlemen, in my dual role as constable and announcer, I now assume the mantle of the latter but only for a brief announcement. Next morning, after my report as a constable, a man and woman from the Ministry of Certain Things were flown in from Battersea by road, with a rug over their knees, that travelled with them Poingggg.
GRAMS	**BUILDING SITE. FADE QUICKLY.**
F.X.	**SCOOPING AWAY EARTH**
MINNIE & HENRY	Niks and Nacks (*extended*).
CRUN	What are you doing Min? The dog's had four bones already, three of them mine, I tell you. Ahh, look another one . . . . Ahh look!
MINNIE	Oh, Lord Crun . . . . This skull is five-million years old.
HENRY	(*sings*) Happy Birthday to you, Happy Birthday to you, Happy Birthday dear Min, Happy Birthday to you.
MINNIE	Thank you Hen, it's nice of you to remember my skull. Now dig on, dig on.
CRUN	**LABOURS ON GRUNTING.**
F.X.	**WITH THE ABOVE: DIGGING**
CRUN	Min, stop wallpapering my trousers while I'm straining with the trowel.
MINNIE	You must get a new pair then — the paint's coming off the knees.
CRUN	I can't understand it you know, those knees were hand-painted by Annagooney.
TAFFY	Sir, will you be long in your excavations, only the workmen are waiting to start work on their tea break you see.
CRUN	No no no. This is a vital brown archeological site sir, it could be that on this very spot, the first men existed, you see this we dug up just now? Do you recognise it?
BILL	It appears to be a piece of mud.
MINNIE	And there's more where that came from!

BILL	Now look, I may be ignorant —
MINNIE	I'm sure you are.
BILL	I will turn a deaf eye to all that nonsense. I was saying I don't see the archeological importance of mud.
MINNIE & HENRY	Morning, morning, morning, morning.
CRUN	Oh No . . . . Here comes Professor Ned Quartermess.
MINNIE	Whoopee!
ORCHESTRA	**I WANT TO BE HAPPY 2/4 FAST**
NED QUARTERMESS	Hello folks it's me, Ned Quartermess, son of a scientist and daughter of darkness, two for the price of one . . . . Hup Hoi.

GRAMS	**OVATION**
QUARTERMESS	Stop!! Now what's all this about, what, what, what?
HENRY	Look at that! Somethings under the ground.
F.X.	**TAPPING**
QUARTERMESS	I's hard, here hold my coconut tree while I have a look. This is a job for those sons of fun, the Army.
ORCHESTRA	**REGAL FANFARE**
HARRY	Ladies and Gentlemen, His Excellency, Rifleman Dene of the 3rd Collapsing Fusiliers.
ORCHESTRA	**PANTOMIME MURMURS**
HARRY	His Grovelling Excellence Sergeant Sir Tom Flar of the 2nd Royal Army of Gooners.
ORCHESTRA	**MURMURS**
HARRY	And now, Miss Stomach Trouble of 1958, Major Denis Bloodnok OBE and Bar.
ORCHESTRA	**NEW BLOODNOK THEME: REGAL**
GRAMS	**EXPLOSION**
BLOODNOK	Will I never be free of them! Oh dear! Now then, what's the trouble?
QUARTERMESS	Unexploded German bomb.
BLOODNOK	What!
GRAMS	**WHOOSH**
BLOODNOK	(*calls from miles off*) Don't get frightened lads! Soon have it safe . . . . Sergeant Spinewait . . . . dig it up with dig.
OMNES	**COCKNEY MOANS etc. 'Cor I don't know I . . . .'**
GRAMS	**DIGGING**
QUARTERMESS	(*over digging*) Thus with ten men holding one million shovels, they dug away in the direction of the thinggggggg.
ORCHESTRA	**HORROR CHORD**
F.X.	**DIGGING GOES THROUGH ORCHESTRA AND GRAMS**
GRAMS	**OSCILLATIONS**
QUARTERMESS	As they dug the thing took shape, twenty-foot long. Red, as large as an engine-boiler, with an entrance on the side, and a sealed compartment in the front.
MINNIE	Ohh dear, dear, dear.
HENRY	I don't like the look of it.
QUARTERMESS	We can't change it now, it's the only one we've got.
HENRY	Yes there is something in what you say.

QUARTERMESS	Yes, it can happen to the best of us.
HENRY	Indeed it can.
QUARTERMESS	Yes, well that seems to have explored that argument in full, doesn't it?
HENRY	But what is this thing?
MINNIE	(sings) Called love . . . e . . . e . . . (whistles etc.).
HENRY	Cease that power singing and stop flashing your insteps, Min!
QUARTERMESS	Well we can't stand round here doing nothing, people will think we're workmen.
BLOODNOK	Laddies, how's the work going on that silly, harmless old bomb eh? You were all frightened of nothing you know.
QUARTERMESS	This line the Major spoke from inside a suit of armour, inside a Cromwell tank.
BLOODNOK	Do you like it? I wear it all the time during explosions you know.
SPIKE	It must be hell in there.
BILL	In my capacity as Announcer I will say this: During the night those concerned continued their digging — Fertanggg!
F.X.	**A HOT BREAK ON VARIOUS SIZED TEMPLE-BLOCKS**
HENRY	MUTTERS (in time with above). There's no doubt about these rhythm skulls Min, they are fifty-million years old.
BLOODNOK	Nonsense! In my opinion these skulls were dropped by the Germans in 1943.
QUARTERMESS	Unexploded German skulls? I hadn't thought of that.
BLOODNOK	Elephant soup with squodged spuds.
QUARTERMESS	I hadn't thought of that either.
BLOODNOK	Sabrina in the Bath.
QUARTERMESS	(chuckles) I do have some spare-time.
F.X.	**DOOR OPENS**
SPIKE	I don't think she has.
MINNIE	Gentlemen, Gentlemen, look . . . . From the bones we discovered I have reconstructed an Irish Stew.
QUARTERMESS	And this is what prehistoric Irish Stews look like?
MINNIE	Yes.
BLOODNOK	I knew it! I knew it! We're all descended from Irish Jews. Oi Vay.
GRAMS	**MATE: SCREAMS AND YELLS OF HELP MIXED WITH QUATERMASS OSCILLATIONS: SPEED DISC UP AND DOWN**
QUARTERMESS	Listen, someone's screaming in agony — fortunately I speak it fluently.

WILLIUM	Oh sir. Ohh me krills are plurned.
QUARTERMESS	Sergeant Fertangg, what's up? Your boots have gone grey with worry.
WILLIUM	I was inside the thing, pickin' up prehistoric fag-ends, when I spots a creature crawling up the wall. It was a weasel, suddenly it went ....
F.X.	**POP**
QUARTERMESS	What a strange and horrible death.
WILLIUM	Then I hears a 'issing sound and a voice say .... 'minardor'.
QUARTERMESS	Minardor? We must keep our ears, nose and throat open for anything that goes Minardor.
HENRY	Be forewarned Sir, the Minardor is an ancient word, that can be read in the West of Ministers Library.
QUARTERMESS	It so happens I have Westminster Library on me and, Gad, look there I am inside examining an occult dictionary.
F.X.	**THUMBING PAGES**
QUARTERMESS	Minardor, minardor m . . . m . . m . Min Min Min, Min Min.
MINNIE	Yes yes, yes yes yes.
QUARTERMESS	I feel an attack of Conks coming on . . . . quick Brandyyyyy.
F.X.	**BOOTS**
MAX	Now you know the power of my conk.
MAX & ORCHESTRA	**MUSIC** (*Applause*)
BILL	Meantime, Professor Quartermess is endeavouring to open the front compartment.
QUARTERMESS	Now workmen I want you to drill through this place here you see. Now you're sure you know all about using micro-Radium tipped drills for non-porous surfaces?
ECCLES	Yer yer all dat . . . . I know all dat. (*rubbish*)
QUARTERMESS	Right.
ECCLES	O.K. den, switch on . . . .
GRAMS	**HUM OF GENERATOR . . . . WHIRL OF DRILL . . . . THEN COLOSSAL SHORTING OF ELECTRICITY.**
ECCLES	(*over above sound*) Owwwwwwwwww.
QUARTERMESS	Are you sure you know what you're doing?
ECCLES	Yer, but I'm willing to take a second opinion.
QUARTERMESS	Look there's a hole appearing!
ECCLES	Let me have a look . . . . Ohhhhhhh.

QUARTERMESS	What can you see?
ECCLES	A glass-eye.
QUARTERMESS	What's the matter, doesn't he trust you? I say (*sniffs*) can you smell something?
ECCLES	Yer.
QUARTERMESS	(*sniff*) Major Bloodnok?
ECCLES	No, dis smells like Irish Stew.
QUARTERMESS	Gad! My brain raced into various directions, the frontal lobes to Charing Cross and the Isle of Rhyl to the Antipodes . . . . the smell ties up with Minnie's replica of the Irish Stew . . . . Break that door down, with this break.
GRAMS & F.X.	**LONG SERIES OF SMASHING DOOR DOWN. GOES ON AND ON . . . . GIVE IT VARIATION IN KIND. I.E. FIRST CONFIDENT CRASHES ON DOOR WITH AXE. THESE ALL VERY LONG. FAIL THEN RENEWED. THEN FURIOUS. . . . THEN FRENZIED . . . . THEN HEAVY FULL BLOODED BLOWS. . . . FURIOUS SAWING . . . . THEN HAMMERING ON DOOR WITH FISTS . . . . MAD RATTLING OF THE DOOR KNOB . . . . THEN FOUR OR FIVE HEAVY BLOWS . . . . THEN A MAD FURIOUS HATCHET ATTACK ON THE DOOR.**
ECCLES	I know when I'm beaten . . . .
QUARTERMESS	Hold this coconut-tree . . . . let me try . . . .
F.X.	**DOOR OPENS. SOUND OF HINGE**
QUARTERMESS	It was open all the time. Dear listeners, inside the sealed compartment, were the complete skeletons of three serge-suits along with the bones of a bowler hat.
HENRY	Min, go and preserve these specimens in brown-fume spirit and quilled-leather Ong . . . .
MORIARTY	I say: Who's that? What's that light?

GRYTPYPE-THYNNE	It's daylight.
MORIARTY	Oh lovely, lovely. Have you any food, have you some food down there, any nice food . . . any spoiled chips and things?
QUARTERMESS	Who is that hovering on the stairs?
GRYTPYPE-THYNNE	That is the Great International Leaper and Balloonist extraordinary, Le Comte Viscomte de Comte Jim 'Winds'. . . .
F.X.	**WIND ESCAPING FROM A BALLOON**
GRYTPYPE-THYNNE	. . . . Moriarty. Known as the Mantovani of Piccadilly. There he goes.
QUARTERMESS	Gad, time for Ray Ellington and the old brandyyyyyyyy.
GRAMS	**MAD RUSH AWAY OF BOOTS**
RAY	Man! The introductions he gives me . . . .
RAY ELLINGTON QUARTET	**MUSIC**
	(*Applause*)
RAY	Melodies from Old Ireland. (*going off*)
QUARTERMESS	There he goes the Webster Booth of Ghana.
BILL	We are now approaching the climax of this thrilling serial in one-part. Around the great scarlet capsule the entire cast are assembled. That's me in the wig.

QUARTERMESS	My friends. We have just one hour to find out the origin of this Giant Skrimpsonskrampson, after that they are letting the press in.
BLUEBOTTLE	Yes, hurry up man, I am waiting for a headline.
QUARTERMESS	Gad, it's a trilby hat on legs!
BLUEBOTTLE	Steady my man, I am Ace Bluebottle, known in Fleet Street as Scoop Bluebottle, wonder-boy reporter.
QUARTERMESS	What paper do you represent?
BLUEBOTTLE	Brown Paper. What is the weekly organ of the Finchley Beat Generation, Editors Bluebottle & Bluebottle. Headline . . . . Boy Reporter Bluebottle scoops. F.X. TYPEWRITER BEHIND. Headline . . . . From under the nose of Lord Beaverbrook, Flash!! Giant German Bomb a hoax, 'I did it in my spare time' Says Sydenham night watchman. Sittin' in his watchman's hut greyheaded sixty-seven year old Tom Onions of Pukers Lodge Mon., said 'It all come so easy in the dark hours'.
ECCLES	Your makin' it up.
BLUEBOTTLE	Silence man! Bend down!
F.X.	**RIP**
BLUEBOTTLE	Oh, It's Professor Eccles . . . . the brains behind . . . .
ECCLES	What? What's that?
BLUEBOTTLE	The brains behind the Windscale disaster . . . . Scoop! Prof. Eccles gives the Brown Paper Daily exclusive statement . . . .

ECCLES	What what what.
BLUEBOTTLE	Can I quote you on dat please?
ECCLES	No. My 'what what what's' are private.
BLUEBOTTLE	Well give us an exclusive statement.
ECCLES	O.K. then, I like chips in brown gravy.
F.X.	**DIALLING ON PHONE**
BLUEBOTTLE	(*talks over dialling*) Sflashou . . . . helooo? Give me the city desk.
GRAMS	**HARRY (DOUBLE TAPE SPEED) 'Hello City desk here.'**
BLUEBOTTLE	Listen Ed. Scoop! Bottle here, clear the front page.
GRAMS	**HARRY: What for my lad?**
BLUEBOTTLE	Professor Eccles denies Paternity case, 'I like chips in brown gravy he tells the Judge'.
GRAMS	**HARRY: Great work kid, keep it up.**
BLUEBOTTLE	Thanks Ed. Now for the exclusive picture. Professor Quartermess pretends to sing and all the others put your fingers in your ears . . . . Ready . . . . Points super Junior candle Flash gun with cardboard built-in trigger . . . . say cheese . . . .
GRAMS	**FLASH AND COLOSSAL EXPLOSION**
BLUEBOTTLE	Oh . . . . my spons . . . . who's been meddling with my thin equipment.
GRYTPYPE-THYNNE	Gentlemen, the Count and I have the solution to the Red Capsule Thing.

Egg going to work on a man

QUARTERMESS	How do you know?
GRYTPYPE-THYNNE	We just watched the last instalment on the television.
ECCLES	Ha dat reminds me I must pay the last instalment on my television. Ha ha ha ha ha . .
QUARTERMESS	That fell a bit flat didn't it. Try singing it.
ECCLES	Anything to save it. (*sings*) 'Ha dat reminds me I must pay the last instalment on my television set' . . . . ya ha ha ha ha. Nope.
QUARTERMESS	Well try it with full orchestral accompaniment.
ORCHESTRA	**OPERA LIKE TUNE TO FIT THE PHRASE IN QUESTION, WHICH ECCLES SINGS**
F.X.	**JELLY SPLOSH**
GRYTPYPE-THYNNE	Moriarty, try it on the zylophone.
GRAMS	**RED HOT ZYLOPHONE BREAD WITH MORIARTY SINGING ALL SPEEDED UP FROM THREE TO ABOUT FIVE, JELLY SPLOSH.**
MORIARTY	Owwwwwww.
BLOODNOK	Who threw that stuff at the Count?
QUARTERMESS	Gad, look what it is.
BLOODNOK	The phantom strikes again! Ohh . . . . it must be hell in there, and there's obviously more where that came from.
QUARTERMESS	Now it's coming clearer.
BLOODNOK	Is it?
QUARTERMESS	Yes, poltergeists throw stuff about.
SPIKE	They must be in a bad way.
QUARTERMESS	This proves my theory, this Scarlet Capsule is the seat of Spirit beings.
WILLIUM	Sir, the gentlemen of the Press is 'ere. I tried to hold 'em back but they burst through by puttin' money in me hand.
QUARTERMESS	Spoken like a true commissionaire.
F.X.	**JELLY SPLOSH**
QUARTERMESS	He's been stuck by a neolithic Irish Stew, it's the spirits at work again. There's only one answer . . . . Eccles? Prepare a series of TNT charges to destroy the Thing.
ECCLES	RUBBISH.
GRAMS	**SPLOSH (THIS INTERRUPTS ECCLES TALKING RUBBISH)**
QUARTERMESS	Ahh! Another one.

ORCHESTRA	**DRAMA IN EVIL CHORDS**
	and
GRAMS	**QUATERMASS OSCILLATIONS. BIG BEN CHIMES — THE BUILD UP NOTES TO THE ACTUAL STRIKING OF MIDNIGHT. BUT THE FIRST NOTE OF MIDNIGHT IS NOT THE GREAT BOOMING SOUND BUT A VERY TINY 'TING'. (TRIANGLE).**
BILL	All night preparations to explode the thing continued, for miles around people had to be evacuated.
F.X.	**KNOCK ON DOOR: DOOR OPENS**
BREATHY KENSINGTON THING	Yes, what is it?
QUARTERMESS	I'm terribly sorry to knock you up so late.
BREATHY KENSINGTON THING	They all say that.
QUARTERMESS	I'm afraid you'll have to be evacuated.
BREATHY KENSINGTON THING	Oh, well come in, I'll just pack a few things.
QUARTERMESS	Well er . . . I . . .
BILL	At this point the script was heavily censored, but we leave the ensuing silence for the listeners to imagine what followed.
	LONG PAUSE
BLOODNOK	Youuuuuu filthy swine, back to your own beds.
ECCLES	Major, the dynamite's all ready in the Thing.
BLOODNOK	Oh, well tell everybody to take cover.
ECCLES	O.K. Take cover Major.
BLOODNOK	Thank you for telling me lad. Get hold of the plunger lad.
QUARTERMESS	Stop! There's a man called Moriarty tied up inside the Thing.
GRYTPYPE-THYNNE	Yes, yes, I know, it's all right Ned.
QUARTERMESS	All right? He'll be blown to bits.
GRYTPYPE-THYNNE	Don't worry, I have the Count heavily insured against such things.
QUARTERMESS	No, I'm afraid I can't allow you to do such a thing.
GRYTPYPE-THYNNE	Fifty pounds be enough?
QUARTERMESS	Right. Now stand by the plunger . . . . ten 9 8 7 6 5 4 3 er . . . .
ECCLES	(*whispers*) Two.
QUARTERMESS	Two, One. Fire!
	(*pause*)

ECCLES	Huh ha ha ha ha ha I forgot to connect it up.
QUARTERMESS	Get over and fix it then . . . .
ECCLES	*(goes off)* O.K.
QUARTERMESS	And nobody touch that plunger.
F.X.	**DIALLING**
GRYTPYPE-THYNNE	Hello? Imprudential Insurance? Can I take out another one of those policy things? . . . . Eccles . . . . Mad Dan Eccles . . . . yes.
F.X.	**PHONES DOWN**
GRYTPYPE-THYNNE	Another fifty be enough Ned?
QUARTERMESS	Huh.
GRAMS	**EXPLOSION. ECCLES AND MORIARTY YELL AND SCREAM INTO THE SKY. THE EXPLOSION GOES AT NORMAL SPEED BUT MORIARTY AND ECCLES SPEED UP FROM NORMAL**
ANDREW TIMOTHY	This is the Flibbt Dabby dee Service of the BBC. The Giant capsule was today exploded and went . . . . Bang! London Transport experts have however discovered what the Thing was — apparently the remains of the Three Blue Serge suits, found inside, were in fact those of three sit-down tube strikers and the capsule was a Tube Train that had been shunted into a siding and forgotten . . . . the Mystic word 'Minardor' was in fact the word 'Mind the Doors'. Not a very good end, but tidy don't you think . . . . Goodnight.
F.X.	**JELLY SPLOSH**
ANDREW TIMOTHY	Ohhh!
BLOODNOK	And there's more where that came from Tim!
ORCHESTRA	**'I WANT TO BE HAPPY' PLAYOUT**

THE TAY BRIDGE DISASTER

The Goon Show, No. 256 (9th Series, No. 15)
Transmission:
Monday, 9th February 1959: 8.30—9.00 p.m. Home Service
Wednesday, 11th February 1959: 9.30—10.00 p.m. Light Programme
Studio: Camden Theatre, London

It was a stormy nacht, and as the wind rustled through a thousand kilts, the crazed poet Macgoonigal was composing verse and worse. As the fog descends over the gloomy Loch, certain mysterious Eastern gentlemen, employed by Hindu Railways Inc., attempt to remove Ned's mechanical support. The plot fails, but not before the contagious disease Poona Krutt has destroyed 912 Hebridean chickens and Eccles from the waist down. This disaster is recorded in history books with the naming of the new bridge after the well known Indian beverage.

The main characters

Ned Seagoon	Harry Secombe
Moriarty	Spike Milligan
Grytpype-Thynne	Peter Sellers
Eccles	Spike Milligan
Hairy Scot	Peter Sellers
MacThroat	Spike Milligan
Wolfit	Spike Milligan
Major Denis Bloodnok	Peter Sellers
Willium	Peter Sellers
Macgoonigal	Peter Sellers
Jim	Spike Milligan
Minnie Bannister	Spike Milligan
Pandit Banerjee	Spike Milligan
Dr Tookrum	Peter Sellers
Bluebottle	Peter Sellers

The Ray Ellington Quartet
Max Geldray
Orchestra conducted by Wally Stott
Announcer: Wallace Greenslade
Script by Spike Milligan
Produced by John Browell

THE TAY BRIDGE DISASTER

BILL	This is the BBC Light Programme. Tiddey pong.
SEAGOON	And now the same thing in Aramaic. Tiddey pong.
GRAMS	**PETER AND SPIKE Ping tar nat plung tar fern tule, knin, querdge, harat, Hume. DURING THE RECORDING PETER & SPIKE HIT A COW BELL, TEMPLE BLOCK, BLOW A WHISTLE DUCK CALL (PLAY FAST).**
BILL	It sounds naughty.
SEAGOON	It is.
MORIARTY	And there's more where that came from —
F.X.	**COLOSSAL SLAPSTICK**
MORIARTY	SHRIE K.
GRYTPYPE-THYNNE	Back you fumed frog of a man.
SEAGOON	Mr Greenslade, clutch the shins, and announce this announcement on the wireless set.
BILL	*(megaphone)* Hello England.
ECCLES	*(off)* Hello . . .
BILL	I give up. *(goes off muttering).*
PETER	*(megaphone)* Snatching up his dying announcement Ned continues Aye!
SEAGOON	*(megaphone)* Hello folks, leather speaking trumpet announcement in the modern wireless talking manner. To celebrate the 200th anniversary of Burns, Cuts and Bruises, we go over to the Krutty-Crab ridden seashore of the Scotland.
ORCHESTRA	**DRONE CHORDS. CHISHOLM PLAYS TATTY TROMBONE BAGPIPE MELODY. (AD LIB) CHISHOLM DECIDES TO SING A SCOTS MELODY DEVINE. GRAMS: JELLY SPLOSH. CHISHOLM CONTINUES TO PLAY TROMBONE, ALMOST IMMEDIATELY. F.X. PISTOL SHOT. GEORGE: Och Nigger nag the noo. F.X. CLANG OF TROMBONE HITTING THE GROUND.**

ORCHESTRA	**REVERT TO VERY FAST TATTY 'I WANT TO BE HAPPY' PLAYOFF. GREAT CYMBAL SMASH AT THE END, CYMBAL FALLS TO THE GROUND. F.X. DROP A LOAD OF CYMBALS TO BOOST IT.**
HAIRY SCOT	Hernia, the nig eertt the noon letn thee noonnn.
MATCHROAT	Ocgghhh.
SEAGOON	Hello, hello hello, Ned, calling on his Mac Megaphone made from red Scottish hairs folks. These sounds were the dreaded sounds of the Phantom Trombonist of the Glen.
HAIRY SCOT	Ayeeeee they do say it's the ghost of George Chisholm's grandfather, killed one stormy night when the Tay Bridge died.
GEORGE	That's troo, real troo, I was killed outright, the noo!
SEAGOON	Thank you George Chisholm and his phoney Scots accent!
GEORGE	*(rage)* Oi Vay Mon Nigger nang the noon.
SEAGOON	There he goes folks, he and speaking part fee of two guineas.
WOLFIT	And now! The tale . . . 'twas a dark and windy night . . .
GRAMS	**WIND HOWLS IN.**
BLOODNOK	*(off)* Ohhhhhhhhh!
WOLFIT	. . . and as far as the eye could see it was 1878 and *(self fade)* the krins were . . .
GRAMS	**WIND HOWLS. EXPLOSION (DISTANT).**
BLOODNOK	Ohhhh so soon in the programme . . . ohhhhh.
SEAGOON	In the year 1878 I had a bridge building company in Suckeyhall Street, I didn't have an office but I did have a suckeyhall Street — ha ha ho he ho!
GRAMS	**MIX IN TERRIBLE MASS CROWDS BRAWL. SMASHING GLASS, SCREAMS, DISTANT BAGPIPE AT SPEED.**
SEAGOON	Hear that? Celtic versus the Rangers.
HAIRY SCOT	Aye! While half Scotland crammed the Fotbaw Stadium, Ned dillingently went about building up his business.
SEAGOON	*(sings)* 'I belongs to Glasgow' *(talks)* Ice Creams, fotbaw badges, bandages, guns, clubs. *(sings)* 'Dear old Glasgow town'.
F.X.	**PENNY IN A TIN CUP**
SEAGOON	Thank you sir, a dud Burmese sixpence? Scotland for ever sir!
RAY	Och Aye and Oi Vay Mon, it's a warum bracht moonlacht nacht for the Schidduch the noo mon.
SEAGOON	And Bless old Ghana too!
RAY	Folks, I don't know how I get these parts, I just don't know.

110

MAX	What about me boy? Dey got me down as a Chinese.
RAY	Man, you won't get away wid it.
MAX	I know boy, it's the old Conk that gives me away.
SEAGOON	Never mind Max, it keeps the rain of yer tie mate.
MAX	Yes! Dat conk is working for me boy, Ploogie!
WILLIUM	'Old it, 'old on yer, what's all this? An Englishman, Irishman and a Jew? Wot you a doin' of then.
SEAGOON	We're just posing for a joke.
WILLIUM	Can't you read that hairy sign mate? 'No Posin' for English, Irish or Jewish jokes on even dates. Lift up yer 'at!
F.X.	**RESOUNDING WHACK ON HEAD**
SEAGOON	*(Scream).*
WILLIUM	Now sign this receipt for that lump I just gid yer.
GRAMS	**SHORT HOT XYLOPHONE BREAK**
SEAGOON	There.
WILLIUM	Wassis? Maureen Shag? That yourn name?
SEAGOON	No, that's the name of my signature.
GRAMS	**SMASH AND GRAB RAID IN MIDDLE DISTANCE. SHOP WINDOW SMASHES. POLICE WHISTLE TOOTING.**
WILLIUM	'Ark on it? It's the sound of a pea vibrating inside a metal cylinder agitated by human wind known to the outside world as a Rozzers Flute or a Narks Lullabye. 'Ere them criminals don't arf lead us a dance.
SEAGOON	Take your partners for the smash and grab one step!
GRAMS	**OLD PRE-ELECTRIC RECORDING OF A BAND PLAYING A ONE STEP. MIX IN COPPERS CROOKS POLICE WHISTLES. OCCASIONAL WHACK ON HEAD. FADE UNDER.**

111

SEAGOON	Gad what a night that was . . . !
GRYTPYPE-THYNNE	You dance devinely little hybrid fellow.
SEAGOON	You must be Lou Praeger.
GRYTPYPE-THYNNE	Ha ha ha oh you devil. Is that your barrel organ outside?
SEAGOON	Yes.
GRYTPYPE-THYNNE	Drive me to the millionaire's entrance to the Unemployment Exchange.
SEAGOON	Splendid it's his turn on the barrel organ.
GRAMS	**TAXI FLAG DOWN**
GRYTPYPE-THYNNE	Step on it!
SEAGOON	So saying he threw down a dog end.
GRAMS	**MIX A BARREL ORGAN AND A CAR DRIVING AWAY TOGETHER. SPEED UP.**
BILL	Ladies and Gentlemen, the Suckey Hall Labour Exchange.
ORCHESTRA	**SNORING . . .**
MACGOONIGAL	Ohh oh what a glorious sight to see Ten Thousand unemployed Scotsmen All happy and Free. They lay there kipping Row after row and . . .
F.X.	**KNOCK KNOCK KNOCK ON DOOR**

MACGOONIGAL	Ohhh? oh ah? *(all snoring stops as though in panic)*
MORIARTY	Everybody quiet — who's there who's dat there? Is it work?
GRYTPYPE-THYNNE	No it's me, Thynne. Friend of the weary.
F.X.	**DOOR OPENS**
SEAGOON	The door was opened by a heavily strained wreck wearing the string remains of an ankle length vest, a secondhand trilby and both feet in one sock.
MORIARTY	And there's more where that came from. I'm a true son of France, I . . . *(screams over following)*
F.X.	**SLAPSTICK**
GRYTPYPE-THYNNE	Ned, this is the great French revolutionary shop-steward and rifle-range target Count Jim Le 'Steamnuts' . . .
GRAMS	**BURST OF STEAM**
F.X.	**BURST OF STEAM AND CASTANETS**
GRYTPYPE-THYNNE	. . . Moriarty. Men of the Royal Labour Exchange, I have good news. I have had talks with the Prime Minister and he has granted us a further extension of unemployment.
ORCHESTRA & GRAMS	**CHEERS**
MACGOONIGAL	And as the Highlanders did shout hooray Max Conks Geldray was seen for to play.

SEAGOON	Hooray, time for Brandy!
GRAMS	**GREAT RUSHING AWAY OF BOOTS**
MAX & ORCHESTRA	**MUSIC**

(applause)

GRAMS	**WAVES ON ROCKY COAST. SEA BIRDS CIRCLING & SQUEALING.**
BILL	From a rocky ledge on Skilla Brae I announce part two. Why I am on a rocky ledge on Skilla Brae I just don't know, I am but a humble announcer, and these sea-birds are no respector of persons.
GRAMS	**SNORING AND DISTANT BAGPIPES**
SEAGOON	*(mouth noises)* Three blissful months I spent in the Labour Exchange, and then one day!
F.X.	**PHONE RINGS**
MORIARTY	Owwwww . . . the phone it's ringing.
GRYTPYPE-THYNNE	You fumed frog, I thought you told me that that phone was unemployed. Ned, you take it, it might be the fiend at work.
F.X.	**PHONE OFF HOOK**
SEAGOON	Don't worry chaps, they'll never know . . . *(Jewish)* Hello, Israeli Embassy Golders Green here.
JIM	Hello is that the Scottish Labour Exchange?
SEAGOON	Yes. Ahhhhh.
JIM	Listen Jim. Listen Jimmmmmmmmmm!
SEAGOON	I'm listening Jimmmmmmmmmmm!
JIM	Is that Seagoon the famous bridge-builder.
SEAGOON	Yes indeed. My name has spread from the little basement I work in, to the old lady next door and back again.
JIM	Come to this address at once Jim it means money . . . Moneeeyy.
SEAGOON	*(mad)* Money!
GRYTPYPE-THYNNE	Money.
GRAMS	**WHOOSH WITH SCREAM OF THYNNE & HARRY GOING WITH IT**
BILL	From a straight Jacket at the bottom of the Thames, I announce a meeting of the Glasgow L.C.C.
GRAMS	**FADE IN SCOTTISH REEL DANCERS WHOOPS, YELLS, MUSIC ACCOMPANIMENT BY A TYPICAL SCOTTISH BAND. OCCASIONAL SMASHED GLASS, OCCASIONAL DRUNKEN YELL.**
HAIRY SCOT	Oh ha ha ha ha, oh that's enough the noo . . . what's the date?

SPIKE	The First of Joone.
HAIRY SCOT	Ay, well we must now declare Hogmanay officially over.
BILL	Hoots Mon sir, the applicants for the new bridge is waiting the noo Och Aye Mon.
HAIRY SCOT	Who's first?
ECCLES	Och Aye me mon. Mac Eccles.
HAIRY SCOT	You ever built bridges before?
ECCLES	Yep, I built the Ummmbababab Bridge in 1867 . . . and I just finished the Forth Bridge.
HAIRY SCOT	When did you build that?
ECCLES	After the first three fell down oh ha ha ha ahhh.
HAIRY SCOT	If it's as old as that gag, I'm not surprised. Well let's hear the plans for the new bridge.
ECCLES	I'll sing it. **GRAMS: TWO PIANOS, BASS & DRUMS VERSION OF MUSIC WHILE YOU WORK** *(sings)* My idea of a Bridge of the River Tay would be made of nice string wood, and string, wid all nice glue, and it would have all dem nails in it . . .
ORCHESTRA	**SOUND OF SCOTTISH SIMMERING RAGE: 'RRRRRRS'.**
HAIRY SCOT	Ah lads, put them claymores away . . . Mr Mac Eccles that Bridge don't soond very good to me.
ECCLES	Well perhaps if I got a better singer to sing it.
HAIRY SCOT	No, it's not your voice or your bridge, it's . . . it's, well it's hard to explain without a mirror.
ECCLES	What what, you all better watch out you Scottish men, or I'll tell you what happened at the ball of Killymuir.
HAIRY SCOT	*(panic)* Stop him lads!
ECCLES	I saw you in haystacks, I saw you in the ricks ha, ha ha and I couldn't hear the music.
GRAMS	**WHOOSH AND JELLY SPLOSH (THE MACREEKIE RISING JELLY SPLOSH)**
HAIRY SCOT	Got him, right in the credentials . . .
SEAGOON	*(megaphone)* Hello hello hello Scottish folks devine, I will now sing and play my own bridge devine. *(sings)* I'll build a bridge of Power, across the River Tay where the dawn comes up like thunder out of China, Cross the Bayyyyy.
ORCHESTRA	**MUTTERS OF SCOTTISH APPROVAL. 'ARRRRRR'.**
SEAGOON	*(sings)* On the road to Bombay where the cross eyed Haggis play down with the English Long Live Bruce hip hip hip hoooooooooorayyyyyyyy.

ORCHESTRA	WILD SCOTTISH APPROVAL. 'ARRRRR HOOTS AR THE NOO'.
GRAMS	ROARS OF APPROVAL
HAIRY SCOT	Seagoon the job is yours . . .
MORIARTY	Stopppppp! Ferme yackabaka le Pune!
GRYTPYPE-THYNNE	I second that . . . let us have fair play, there is still one more bridge to be sung, my client the great French Financial Disaster has this to say . . .
MORIARTY	*(sings)* Sur la' Ponggggg de Avignonnnnnnn, onye danser on yer danserrrrr da d serrrrrrrrrrrrrrrrr.
HAIRY SCOT	Och I must admit his bridge sounds longer.
SEAGOON	I'll sing an extra bit on mine. *(sings)*
BOTH	START A BATTLE OF SING.
GRAMS	MIX TO GRAMS OF SEAGOON & MORIARTY SINGING A DUET. SOUND OF CRICKETS, AND A DISTANT OWL TO INDICATE NIGHT TIME.
GRYTPYPE-THYNNE	*(over)* All through the Steaming Porridge ridden night the two bridge builders extolled their plans in song . . . My Client with his powerful French Bridge against the Might of Seagoons, alas, towards dawn my Client weakened and . . .*(fade)*
GRAMS	TREE STARTS TO FALL. WITH ITS FALL MORIARTY'S VOICE RUNS DOWN AND STOPS AS THE TREE CRASHES TO THE GROUND.
MORIARTY	Curse my weak ankles.
SEAGOON	Hard luck Moriarty.
GRYTPYPE-THYNNE	Congratulations and hatred Ned. All's fair in love and war, let us supply you with the steel for the bridge.
SEAGOON	Have you any samples?
GRAMS	LOAD OF OLD SCRAP POURED OUT
F.X.	DITTO

116

MORIARTY	And there's more where that came from Ned.
SEAGOON	This looks remarkably like Tower Bridge.
GRYTPYPE-THYNNE	You'll get no rubbish from us Ned . . . here, sign the exclusive contract on this bomb . . .
F.X.	**HURRIED WRITING**
GRAMS	**EXPLOSION**
GRYTPYPE-THYNNE	There! Nothing can revoke it — Moriarty? Unchain a fresh Ray Ellington.
F.X.	**CHAINS**
RAY	Man, this is the worst contract I ever had.
RAY ELLINGTON QUARTET	**MUSIC.** *(applause)*
BILL	That was Ray Ellington and his appliances, the applause was recorded by professional mourners. Now, strapped to the railway lines at Paddington, I announce part two . . . The Bridge over the River Tay, the Blasting Operation.
GRAMS	**BLASTING IN ROCK FACE. EXPLOSIONS ROAR OF LOOSE SHALE ETC. AVALANCHING DOWN CLIFF. CRASHING INTO THE RIVER. SOUND OF HOT IRONS DIPPED INTO COLD WATER.**
BLOODNOK	Ohh, thank heaven that's cleared it . . . ohhhh *(calls)* alright lads, it's clear you can come out.
MINNIE	Ohhhhhhhhhhhhh Ohhhhhhhhhhhhhh.
BLOODNOK	What's this black-dress hanging in a tree? What, what is it madam?
MINNIE	I was collecting seagull's eggs up the cliff, there was an explosion . . . Henery went up in the air and I I Oooooooooooo.
F.X.	**VERY VERY HEAVY BODY FALLS TO THE GROUND**
BLOODNOK	Ohhh she's fainted, thank heavens the ground broke her fall. Let me open her handbag and let some of that heavy naughty money out.
F.X.	**COINS BEING COUNTED**
BLOODNOK	Ohhh dee dee deeeee . . . eight nine ten, ten and nine . . . ten and ten . . . pence.
MINNIE	Ohh, where am I?
BLOODNOK	In debt my dear . . .

SEAGOON	Major Bloodnok, why aren't you on the job?
BLOODNOK	This poor female egg-collector fainted from faint and has been struck down in the prime of her 89th year.
MINNIE	Ohhhh, where's Henery?
SEAGOON	He's been buried alive under a thousand tons of earth.
MINNIE	Thank heavens he's safe.
BLOODNOK	She doesn't look very well we must get her to a graveyard as soon as possible.
BILL	Pardon me sir? It's part four.
SEAGOON	We must hurry. Over to part four and meee!
GRAMS	**SEAGOON: Hello folks, it's me, now back to him.**
SEAGOON	Thank you me.
GRAMS	**SEAGOON: Thank me you too.**
MACGOONIGAL	*(approaching)* Oooooooooooooooooöo!
SEAGOON	What's this approaching wearing a transparent kilt?
MACGOONIGAL	That is a special kilt designed for patriotic Scottish Nudists. Tell me sir, is that the new bridge over the Tay.
SEAGOON	Yes, made of solid leather, and due to be opened by Captain Webb who will swim it.
MACGOONIGAL	May I introduce myself, Sir, I am William J. Macgoonigal, poet tradegian and twitt, allow me to pen a verse of appreciation . . . let me get the feel of my tonesss. Ohhhhhh . . .
ORCHESTRA	**Oooooooooooooo.**
MACGOONIGAL	*(continue calls and answers with the Orchestra)* Oh, they're with me tonight.
F.X	**WRITING STARTS**

MACGOONIGAL	Oh beautiful new bridge over the
	    silvery Tay,
	Which has caused the Maharajah of
	    Pongistan to leave his home so far away,
	Incognito in his dress,
	And he will pass this way on his journey
	    to Inverness.

SEAGOON	Jolly good, now, I'll just put the bandage round your eyes. *(calls)* Take aim!
MACGOONIGAL	Just a moment, sir. Underneath the bridge there will travel ships . . . I say, what's that cooking? *(sniff, sniff)* Oh chips.
GRAMS	**WHOOSH**
F.X.	**TUBULAR BELLS HITS THE GROUND**

SEAGOON	He's dropped his Sporran.
PETER & SPIKE	WOGS SINGING.
SEAGOON	'Ello, 'ello, 'ello, what's this approaching? Three Ghee covered Hindus, with revolving knees and a touch of the Poona Krutt.
PANDIT BANERJEE	Hello Hello, man, I'm Pandit Banerjee, this is Doctor Tookrum and that is a Waziri Tribal Chief. *(continues Hindu noises).*
DR TOOKRUM	Hello Mister. I'm Banerjee, we are here shopping for Hindu Railways Incorporated. Pandit Nehru said 'Get out there Banerjee boy and get the European style bridge'. *(continues Indian noises etc.)*
SEAGOON	Oh would you care to stay to dinner?
DR TOOKRUM	Oh my goodness yes.
SEAGOON	Blast. Unfortunately our dinner is at the menders.
PANDIT BANERJEE	A terrible blow, terrible blow. Never mind, I have here a real red-hot ball Curry and Chicken Vindalu!
BLOODNOK	Curry! No! No! — that terrible burning the morning after. No!
RAY	Ohhh Blimey! Bloodnok! you. So we meet again mate!
GRAMS	**EXPLOSION**
BLOODNOK	Oh! It's the Red Bladder, my Mortal enemy from Ferozapore. Put that sword down — I can explain everything.
RAY	*(growls in rage)* Ohhhhhhhhhh . . . You steal three wives from my Harem in 1923 . . . me feel the pinch.
BLOODNOK	Oh! Don't worry Mullah they're all still in working order. I'll go and get them from my country home . . . Taxi!
GRAMS	**TAXI ROARS OFF**
BILL	On the Morrow the first train was to pass over the Bridge, but that night plotters were at work. Tittley ti toe Fertanggggg . . .
GRAMS	**DISTANT OWL. OCCASIONAL CRICKET CHIRPS. DISTANT CHURCH BELL CHIMES.**
BLUEBOTTLE	Pssssttttttt.
ECCLES	What, whattttt. Who dats behind dat bush?
BLUEBOTTLE	Black Hawk, demon bridge-destroyer.
ECCLES	You got the dynamite?
BLUEBOTTLE	Yes. Dis will cost you a pretty penny!

ECCLES	I ain't got a pretty penny!
BLUEBOTTLE	Well, two ugly ones will do then.
SEAGOON	Oi! You two spotty herberts.
ECCLES	Owwwww it's Ned, and he's got his hat on.
BLUEBOTTLE	Hands up, Ned Man, dat does not frite us.
SEAGOON	Blast! Give me that silly bit of twig.
BLUEBOTTLE	Fool this twig contains a torch battery that releases a paralysing electric shock. Screngeee . . . it will go, touch the end and see.
SEAGOON	There — ha ha!
GRAMS	**GREAT SHORT CIRCUIT ELECTRICITY FLASHING FROM POINT-TO-POINT. HARRY: (OVER THIS. YELLS LIKE MAD 'OWWWW HELPPPPPPPPPP YEYEOWOWWW').**
BLUEBOTTLE	Cor, it's a good job it wasn't switched on.
ECCLES	He's passed out . . . and it suits him.
BLUEBOTTLE	Come Mad Dan, while it's dark we must saw down that bridge.
F.X.	**SAWING**
BLUEBOTTLE	Phew! Dis girder is tough.
RAY	Man, dats my leg.
ECCLES	Oh? Who are you den?

MAN GOING TO WORK ON AN EGG

RAY	I don't know, it's too dark to see.
BLUEBOTTLE	'Ere you ever been married to Rita Hayworth?
RAY	No.
BLUEBOTTLE	It's alright Eccles, he's one of us.
RAY	Me got 800 wives.
ECCLES	You better sit down.
BLUEBOTTLE	Come on, I set the dynamite to go off at dawn. He he he. I do feel mean Eccles.
ORCHESTRA	**LINKS**
BILL	Strapped down in a trough filled with sulphuric acid, I announce part six. The Denouément at Dawn.
GRAMS	**VERY TATTY DISTANT BRASS BAND PLAYING APPROPRIATE BRIDGE OPENING MUSIC. TRAIN GOES PUFFING OFF. CHEERS OF CROWD. EXPLOSION OF DYNAMITE. GREAT CRASH AS BRIDGE FALLS INTO THE RIVER. HISSING OF STEAM RUBBLE ETC. GRADUALLY STOPS.**
ECCLES	Well, dats dat!
ORCHESTRA	**LONG SERIES OF TA RA CHORDS — WITH CYMBAL SNAP INTO: 'OLD COMRADES MARCH' PLAYOUT.**

THE GOLD·PLATE ROBBERY

The Goon Show, No. 257 (9th Series, No. 16)

Transmission:

Monday, 16th February 1959: 8.30—9.00 p.m. Home Service

Wednesday, 18th February 1959: 9.30—10.00 p.m. Light Programme

Studio: Camden Theatre, London

Early spring, and the gardens of Seagoon Towers are resplendent with croci and manure. Over the tea-cups the dulcet 'hooray' tones of Lady Lavinia Seagoon can be heard reprimanding her two idiot sons Bazil and Rodney. This idyllic scene changes dramatically to torrid, sweaty Fort Sidi Bel Abbes near Marrakesh, where our hero Lord Seagoon, lately arrived by taxi, is impersonating Arabs to amuse the chickens. Together with the combined forces of Knackers Yard, Interpox and East Finchley Women's Institute, he is to search for arch Villain and bus driver extraordinary, Count Jim 'Scroobs Surprise'... Moriarty, and the missing gold cuspidors.

The main characters

Lord Ned (Roger/Rodney) Seagoon	Harry Secombe
Eccles	Spike Milligan
Lady Lavinia Seagoon	Peter Sellers
Bazil Seagoon	Spike Milligan
Throat	Spike Milligan
Grytpype-Thynne	Peter Sellers
Moriarty	Spike Milligan
Police Constable	Peter Sellers
Willium	Peter Sellers
Major Denis Bloodnok	Peter Sellers
Bluebottle	Peter Sellers

The Ray Ellington Quartet
Max Geldray
Orchestra conducted by Wally Stott
Announcer: Wallace Greenslade
Script by Spike Milligan
Produced by John Browell

THE GOLD·PLATE ROBBERY

BILL	This is the BBC.
HARRY	Gad, it sounds as young as ever, even more so.
PETER	Jove, you're right Nules, say it again Wireless Man.
BILL	This is the BBC Light Programme.
HARRY	It makes you glad to be alive, strengthens the shins, and diminishes the Spon.
PETER	By Jupiter, you're right I'll warrant 'ee. Tell us little Establishment Unit, who invented the BBC Light Prog?
BILL	A Midlothian hedonist, one Mr Arthur Cack OBE, one of England's unsung heroes.
PETER	Did he? Then he won't get away with it, I'll warrant you.
GRAMS	**OVATION**
SEAGOON	Stop folks; Hello folks, this is Neddie folks. Ting-a-ling, ah the telephone folks.
F.X.	**PHONE TAKEN OFF HOOK**
ECCLES	Hello?
SEAGOON	Hello?
ECCLES	Snap.
SEAGOON	Splendid, ring again tomorrow and we'll have another game.
BILL	That vacuous little cameo was in the nature of an entrée to the main steaming ning-nong, plitt platt toof tangg. Ladies and Gentlemen, the Kleens of Blenchinghall, the story of an ordinary English comedy half-hour.
ORCHESTRA	**STATELY HOME THEME — HELD UNDER**

125

PETER	*(as cocky pipe-smoking Englishman)* Hello, my name is, *(mumbles)* Smarmnelyby nera, a , a I want to tell you about the illustrious Seagoons. He was an ordinary Welsh crofter's son who became a very ordinary Prime Minister, joined the Coldstreams at the outbreak of the Armistice and rose to the rank of Private. Let us go back to that ecstatic spring of June, 1887, *(fading)* when all . . . *(mumbles)*.
ORCHESTRA	**FLUTE & BIRDS SONG IN SPRINGTIME THEME**
GRAMS	**TWITTERING BIRDS IN A SURREY WOOD, HORSE CANTERS UP THE GRAVEL DRIVE**
SEAGOON	Tally Ho, hoi, yoicks, gone away, address not known . . . some fox ha ha ha . . . where is that lazy old Irish groom, O'Blast?
RAY	Here I is yo Lordship.
SEAGOON	Oh, Ellington, how many times must I tell you not to stand in the shade, you ruin the colour-scheme. Now, where's me Lady Lavinia Seagoon?
RAY	She's in the great granite Baronial dining-hall.
SEAGOON	What's she doing?
RAY	Eatin' chips.
SEAGOON	Chips? Ah, ha ha, she must be practising for dinner time. Drive me there.
GRAMS	**CAR STARTS UP — STOPS IMMEDIATELY**
SEAGOON	Thank you Ellington. Mother? . . . . Mother? . . . . Oh Mummy?
LADY SEAGOON	What is it Roger darling?
SEAGOON	Oh Daddy, what are you doing at home?
LADY SEAGOON	I live here, and I'm Mummy not Daddy, you've got to know the difference some time.
SEAGOON	Gad, this revelation makes me a man of the world, no more short trousers for me.
LADY SEAGOON	Excused shorts. Oh how proud your father would have been. Now tell me all about the fox-hunt.
SEAGOON	It was wonderful mother. A beautiful spring morning, flowers blooming, and blood everywhere. Oh it's grand to be in England.
BAZIL SEAGOON	Hello mother, hello Rodney . . . by Jove, I'm dashed hungry.
LADY SEAGOON	Bazil darling, where's your chin gone?
BAZIL	I've never had one Mummy.
LADY SEAGOON	You poor thing . . . Ahh what a morning Bazil, the first spring oak-trees pushing their branches up through the lawn.
SEAGOON	Not again, they did the same thing last year.
LADY SEAGOON	I know, it's such a bore isn't it. Let's have tea.

GRAMS	**GREAT CLANGING OF CHURCH BELLS OF VARIOUS SIZES ALL CONCENTRATED**
F.X.	**DOOR OPENS**
THROAT	Who rang dem bells?
SEAGOON	I did, serve tea Jeeves.
THROAT	*(growls)* I'll give you tea.
F.X.	**SMASHING OF A LARGE TEA SET, SPOONS AND ALL ACCOUTREMENT**
LADY SEAGOON	Ohhh dear . . . help *(all over above)*. Rodney, speak to him!
SEAGOON	Hello, Jeeves, I see that Barnsley took another bashin' on Saturday.
F.X.	**GREAT SMASH ON NED'S HEAD WITH GIANT PLATE**
SEAGOON	Ohh that does it. Jeeves, I'm giving you a week's notice.
LADY SEAGOON	Are you mad? Servants are so hard to get.
SEAGOON	Jeeves, I'm giving you twenty-years notice.
THROAT	I quit . . . I just won the pools.
F.X.	**DOOR SLAMS**
SEAGOON	No tea, very well, we'll have . . .
ORCHESTRA & OMNES	**BRANDYYYYY**
GRAMS	**RUNNING CROWD OF BOOTS AND WHOOPS OF DELIGHT**
MAX	Dis can only mean that Geldray is left holding the conk boy.
MAX & ORCHESTRA	**MUSIC**
	(Applause)
GRAMS	**RETURN OF GREAT RUNNING BOOTS**
BILL	*(gasping)* Just made it . . . Part two, a vacancy filled.
F.X.	**KNOCK ON DOOR — DOOR OPENS**
SEAGOON	What do you want?
GRYTPYPE-THYNNE	Lord Seagoon?
SEAGOON	Yes, and I have a licence to prove it.
GRYTPYPE-THYNNE	My friend and I were in Edgware, taking the waters of the horse-trough, when we observed this advert in the London Gazette, and I quote 'Wanted, Butler with complete Tea-Service.'
SEAGOON	Yes, that's mine.

GRYTPYPE-THYNNE	Why is it in the obituary column?
SEAGOON	It's 3d. a line cheaper in there. Are you applying for the vacancy?
MORIARTY	Yes we are. We want to work in the food department where there's food, nice food.
SEAGOON	Pardon me, but that old hat-stand appears to be animate.
GRYTPYPE-THYNNE	You do him a disservice sir, that hat-stand is the *bona fide* remains of what was once the great Count Jim 'Strains-Supreme' . . .
F.X.	**VICIOUS OIL DRUM WITH THE WAX STRING. VICIOUS TONE TEMPLE BLOCKS. RATTLE, BRIEF.**
GRYTPYPE-THYNNE	. . . Moriarty, last of the great butlers. He has waited at table bus-stops and YWCA windows. Hit him with this beater.
SEAGOON	Right.
ORCHESTRA	**GREAT CHINESE GONG IS WALLOPPED**
MORIARTY	(*over above*) Dinner is served.
SEAGOON	He sounds like a butler. Have you any recommendations?
GRYTPYPE-THYNNE	Of course we have . . . Count, unroll the scrolls and documents!
GRAMS & F.X.	**LOAD OF METALLIC RUBBISH. A DOZEN PING-PONG BALLS BOUNCE ON THE FLOOR, HANDFULS OF MARBLES. OLD BUCKETS.**
MORIARTY	And there's more where that come from.
SEAGOON	Very well, you start work at once, lay the table for the Hunt Banquet. Here's the key to the gold-plate.
MORIARTY	Golddddddddddddd? Ahhhhhhhhh . . .
F.X	**FALL OF BODY**

SEAGOON	Is he unconscious?
GRYTPYPE-THYNNE	No, he's in a food trance. There's only one cure Neddie, a fifteen-course dinner then a drive round the grounds in a car with the gold-plate in a sack.
SEAGOON	What, give you my gold-plate? I don't know you from Adam.
GRYTPYPE-THYNNE	Well we're better dressed. Really sir, don't hesitate, you are dicing with death and our future prosperity.
GRAMS	**HEAVY FEASTING OF TWO MEN. OCCASIONAL GRUNTING OF A PIG EATING AND SNUFFLING. MORIARTY AND GRYTPYPE CAN BE OVERHEARD.**
GRYTPYPE-THYNNE	Ha ha ha ha. How's that Moriarty?
MORIARTY	Ha ha ha I'm feeling a little better now.
GRYTPYPE-THYNNE	Good, good. Another quellth of plitts?
LADY SEAGOON	*(over above)* They've been eating for seventeen hours now.
SEAGOON	Yes yes yes, but they've nearly finished.
GRAMS	**PLATES BEING DROPPED INTO A SACK**
LADY SEAGOON	They're taking my gold-plate.
GRAMS	**CAR DRIVING AWAY**
SEAGOON	It's all right, it's only part of that poor man's cure, Mother. They're only going to drive around the grounds, don't worry. *(fade)* They'll be back in five minutes. Ha ha ha ha . . .
ORCHESTRA	**SHORT CLIPPED CHORD**
POLICE CONSTABLE	And you say it's fifteen years since they stole the gold-plate?
SEAGOON	Yes, fifteen years and three minutes to the day.
POLICE CONSTABLE	How is it you didn't report this sooner?
SEAGOON	I overslept.
POLICE CONSTABLE	I see, yeas . . . Any nut-cases in your family?
SEAGOON	No, mostly leather.
POLICE CONSTABLE	I see, now these gold plates, are they valuable sir?
SEAGOON	Yes, they had food on them.
POLICE CONSTABLE	RIGHT! So that's sixty large gold plates and sixty small . . . anything else?
SEAGOON	Oh yes, one coal sack.
POLICE CONSTABLE	Is it valuable?
SEAGOON	Yes, it's got the plates inside.
F.X.	**PHONE RINGS. PHONE OFF HOOK.**

POLICE CONSTABLE	Bow Street Police Station, criminals done while you wait, Hello . . . Oh it's for you me lord.
SEAGOON	Yes?
ECCLES	Hello?
SEAGOON	Hello?
ECCLES	Snap dat's two games to me.
SEAGOON	Right, you been practisin'?
ECCLES	Yer, dat's why I'm winnin'. Well I better get back.
F.X.	**PHONE DOWN**
POLICE CONSTABLE	Excuse me sir . . . While you were talking, this sludge was dredged up in the English Channel.
MORIARTY	Owwwwwwwwwww!
SEAGOON	What? Search his pockets for salt water.
MORIARTY	It's all a mistake. I'm a female channel swimmer, I tell you . . . here's a record to prove it.
GRAMS	**SPLASH. SEAL BARK. BAGPIPES.**
SEAGOON	You imposter, that's a seal. But why the bagpipes?
MORIARTY	It's the Great Seal of Scotland.
SEAGOON	Now I recognise you by the air you're breathing . . . you're Count Jim Moriarty from the body of the same name. Officer, search that suit, inside you'll find a man, arrest him.
POLICE CONSTABLE	Come on now son, where are them gold plates?
MORIARTY	You can't make me talk.
F.X.	**SLAPSTICK**
MORIARTY	Oh Ha, you've made me talk. I'll tell you Grytpype took all the gold-plate to Algiers.
SEAGOON	Spain . . . Taxi!
GRAMS	**EXPLOSION**
MAX	Where you going darling?
SEAGOON	Follow that continent, darling.
GRAMS	**CAR DRIVES OFF WITH CHICKENS CLUCKING**
BILL	The combined sound of an automobile and a hen, was especially recorded for motoring enthusiasts who keep chickens. Now part two. A chase across continents. The trail of the gold plates led Lord Seagoon to Marrakesh.
GRAMS	**WOG MUSIC . . . TRIO WITH A FEMALE VOCAL**
F.X.	**CLATTER OF AN EASEL OR SIMILAR**

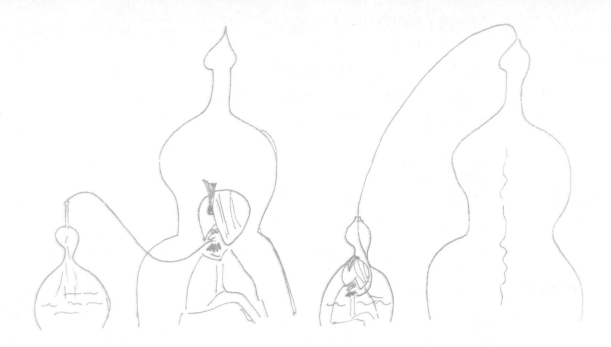

SEAGOON	Opps, I'm terribly sorry . . . sir.
PETER	I should think so too.
SEAGOON	My information led me to a coffee-house, just off the main caravan route, where outside the sun purged the streets of shade. Inside, all was cool and jasymined.
GRAMS	**SWEETER WOG MUSIC. SOUND OF A FOUNTAIN PLAYING.**
SEAGOON	In an Alambrhan tesselated forecourt, a fountain played on the purple water-lilies. Couched in lattice recesses, purdered Tureg beauties attended local sheiks. I was conducted to a low Morrocan coffee-table. My attendant wore the bleached robes of a Nomad arab. His burnoose was contained with a rope of black camel hair, at his waist a curved Hedjez dagger protruded from his cummerbund. He bowed low, touched his forehead in time-honoured Islamic salute and spoke.
WILLIUM	The boiled fish and rice puddin's orf mate.
SEAGOON	I see . . . ahem, your accent is familiar, Oh Arab prince.
WILLIUM	Yernnnn, I went to Kolidge in Kambridge, oh English mate.
SEAGOON	What were you studying?
WILLIUM	Cockney . . . I got it orf pat.
SEAGOON	Did you?
WILLIUM	He didn't mind.
SEAGOON	Tell me, oh Arab prince, have you ever heard of a Hercules Grytpype-Thynne?
WILLIUM	What's it used for?

SEAGOON	A name, a name called Hercules Grytpype-Thynne.
WILLIAM	Bit of a mouthful isn't it?
SEAGOON	I agree, but do you know a man who is called by it?
WILLIAM	I knows a bald-headed old woman called Rattler Blotts.
SEAGOON	No, that doesn't sound like him . . .
SPIKE	Hello, hello Ladies and Gentlemen, now then, the management of this club has imported Ray Ellington all the way from London. Take it away, now.
RAY ELLINGTON QUARTET	**MUSIC.**
	(applause)
BILL	During the *marde funilie* of that music, Lord Seagoon greased his boots and slipped away to see the last British Ambassador in Marrakesh.
ORCHESTRA	**BLOODNOK THEME WITH WOG FLUTE LEAD**
GRAMS	**(START BEFORE MUSIC STOPS) THUNDER, LIGHTNING, RAIN ON TIN ROOF DRIPPING INTO A WATER BUTT. SKITTLES ALL BEING KNOCKED OVER BY A BALL IN AN ECHOEY BOWLING ALLEY.**
BLOODNOK	Ohh dear, it's a wonder what the human body can stand up to. Ohh, now for a kip on full Ambassadors pay. Wonder what Gladwyn Jebb's doing.
RAY	*(rage)* Bloodnokkkkkkkkkk!
BLOODNOK	*(falls to pieces)* Ohh.
F.X.	**BITS AND PIECES FALL ON FLOOR**
BLOODNOK	The Red Bladder Oww!
GRAMS	**WHOOSH**
F.X.	**TIN CAN HITS FLOOR**
BLOODNOK	*(miles off)* Go away, or I'll take my wig off.
RAY	Bloodnok, don't be frite mate, I come to do business. Me got money.
GRAMS	**WHOOSH**

BLOODNOK	Ohhhh, you said the secret British password.
RAY	Me want guns, bullets and drip-dry shirts.
F.X.	**UNROLLING MAP**
BLOODNOK	Ohh ha ha, go to this spot on the map, dig upwards for ten feet and you'll find 'em buried up a tree.
RAY	Good. Now here's the payment mate.
BLOODNOK	A gold plate? Ohh, just what I've always wanted for me din-dins.
F.X.	**DOOR BURSTS OPEN**
SEAGOON	Which one of you two men is the British Ambassador?
BLOODNOK	What? Does my Union Jack nightshirt mean nothing to you?
SEAGOON	What's it doing round your ankles?
BLOODNOK	It's been lowered for the night I tell you. It's hell when it's at half-mast.
SEAGOON	Major, I'm on the trail of some stolen gold plates.
BLOODNOK	Stolen??? Are you . . .
F.X.	**A PLATE DROPS TO THE FLOOR, ROLLS ALONG AND ROUND AND ROUND UNTIL IT STOPS**
SEAGOON	*(over above)* A gold plate . . . !
BLOODNOK	Nonsense! That's my Golden Record Award, for me millionth record of . . .
GRAMS	**PIANO PLAYING BY PETER — BLOODNOK SINGING** 'I don't know who you are Sir, or where you come from but you've done me a power of good (EXPLOSION) I don't know who you are Sir, or where you come from but you've done me a power of good. I was standing there Sir, doing up me boot, suddenly from a back street I saw this hairy brute . . . (F.X. PHONE RINGS) BLOODNOK Hello? ECCLES Hello? BLOODNOK Snap, that's got rid of him, sssoooo . . . (sings) I don't know who you are Sir, or where you come from, but you've done me a power of good. (record speeds up) You've done, you've done me . . . a power of (pause) GOOOOOOOODDDDDDDDDD!

SEAGOON	I don't believe it.
RAY	Stop! Me know man who got lot of gold-plate . . . mate. Captain of Foreign Legion, Fort Sidi Bel Abbes mate.
SEAGOON	Right. Seagoon? — yes — Follow that pointed finger darling — right.
GRAMS	**RUNNING BOOTS WITH QUEEN MARY'S HOOTER BOTH DEPARTING AND SPEEDING UP**
BILL	I will now announce the Fort of Sidi Bel Abbes in fluent French, ze Fort at Sidi Bel Abbes in Fluent French.
GRAMS	**MEN MARCHING. DISTANT ORDERS IN FRENCH.**
HARRY	*(French accent)* Mon Captain zere is a bundle of low-grade rags to zee you.
GRYTPYPE-THYNNE	Low-grade rags . . . nonsense!
HARRY	He zays he knew your mother.

GRYTPYPE-THYNNE	Oh Dear.
MORIARTY	Ohhhh Grytpype, my son, your French Daddy.
GRYTPYPE-THYNNE	You steamer, I told you not to hang round me during your lifetime.
MORIARTY	You promised me one of the plates, I demand...
F.X.	**SLAPSTICK**
GRYTPYPE-THYNNE	Sergeant, throw this revolutionary in the Shatt el Arab prison.
HARRY	Come on you.
BOTH	GO OFF PROTESTING ... TAKES A VERY LONG TIME TO GET TO THE DOOR. FINALLY IN THE EXTREME DISTANCE...
GRAMS	**DISTANT SHOTS AND SHOUTS AS ARABS ATTACK**
HARRY	Sacre Bleu, Mon Captain, ze Arabs are ze attacking us? *(English)* Bang Bang.

GRYTPYPE-THYNNE	Bang Bang? So they're shooting at us in English are they. Man the ramparts and any other parts you can get hold of.
ORCHESTRA	**DRAMATIC WAR MUSIC**
GRAMS	**DISTANT SOUND OF THE BATTLE**
BLUEBOTTLE	Bangee, Bangee . . . Bangee. Another Arab crashes down to the rifle-but of Beau Bluebottle, garçon de Legion.
ECCLES	BANG Banggggg . . . Click . . . Oh, a dud.
BLUEBOTTLE	Do you like wars, Eccles?
ECCLES	Yer Vanilla flavoured wars are good.
BLUEBOTTLE	Which side are you on, the Arabs or the Foreign Legion?
ECCLES	I don't know, dere both shooting at me. Why did you join the Legion?
BLUEBOTTLE	It's the same old story mon ami. I joined to forget a woman, Miriam Reene of 33 Croft Street, East Finchley. She turned me down for Dave Freeman.
ECCLES	Oh, was he better looking?
BLUEBOTTLE	He, he, he, no. She said to us . . . at playtime she said, . . . Eccles, don't do dat you'll get into trouble . . . well, at playtime she said to me and Dave. *(puts on voice)* 'Who shows the most gets me'.
ECCLES	You won?
BLUEBOTTLE	No, I only got a bit of string, and he got a fourpence and a saucer of water.
ECCLES	Ohh, some people are born rich.
BLUEBOTTLE	Oh ho hum.
ECCLES	What'd what'd the matter?
BLUEBOTTLE	I haven't had any sleep all night. You know that film 'Room at the Top'?
ECCLES	Yer.
BLUEBOTTLE	Well, I'm in the room underneath 'em.
F.X.	**PHONE RINGS**
ECCLES	Fort Sidi Bel Abbes here, Comme on talivous.
SEAGOON	*(distort as Eccles)* Hello?
ECCLES	Hello?
SEAGOON	Snap.
ECCLES	Oh tres bon.
SEAGOON	That's three games to one, right. Come down and let me in the back door.

GRAMS	**MAD RUSH OF BOOTS DOWN WOODEN STEPS.** **TAKES A LONG TIME.**
F.X.	**DOOR OPENS**
ECCLES	Dey played that record too fast.
SEAGOON	That's it, go on, give all our secrets away.
ECCLES	O.K. Bluebottle's shirts are made from his mum's old drawers.
BLUEBOTTLE	Fermez le bouch vous, Or je will blat vous on le conk. *(confused arguments)*
SEAGOON	Listen little string and teeth soldier, the Captain of this fort is a criminal, so what we are going to do is this . . . *(fade)*
GRYTPYPE-THYNNE	Who's that? Is that you darling?
SEAGOON	*(whispers)* Blast it's Grytpype-Thynne. Leave this to me, I'm a brilliant impressionist. *(chicken clucking).*
GRYTPYPE-THYNNE	A horse? There's no horses in this fort.
SEAGOON	*(whispers) (dog howling).*
GRYTPYPE-THYNNE	There's no chickens either.
ECCLES	*(whispers)* This one's a smart one. Let me try, I'm good at dis.
	SERIES OF MAD NOISES . . . PAUSE.
ECCLES	*(whispers)* Dat fooled him.
SEAGOON	Are you sure?
ECCLES	Dat fooled you, didn't it?
F.X.	**PISTOL SHOT . . . SCREAMS**
GRYTPYPE-THYNNE	So it's Lord Seagoon and Company.
SEAGOON	Where's that gold-plate, mother's wating to serve dinner to some guests, we've been waiting for fifteen years for dinner, and the rumbling sounds are dreadful.
GRYTPYPE-THYNNE	I've had them all melted down into gold bullets and they're in this gun.
F.X.	**SHOTS**
SEAGOON	Oh. Hooray, I'm going to die rich . . . Ohhh.
ORCHESTRA	**TA RAAAAA CHORD**
HARRY	Well, that's it folks, as you all go to the cloaks, you'll be handed back your glass-eyes, false-teeth and wooden-legs, and wouldn't you in two lads . . .
ORCHESTRA	**'OLD COMRADES MARCH' PLAYOUT**

THE £50 CURE

The Goon Show, No. 258 (9th Series, No. 17)
Transmission:
Monday, 23rd February 1959: 8.30—9.00 p.m. Home Service
Wednesday, 25th February 1959: 9.30—10.00 p.m. Light Programme
Studio: Camden Theatre, London

America is about to purchase the British Isles and move them piece-by-piece to Disneyland. Subsequent despair leads to bizarre behaviour within English society. Bloodnok commences a World tuba playing tour of England, Bluebottle is sick, and National Health Doctors prescribe money for the incurable disease, Advanced Poverty. Within this realistic scenario Mr Henry Crun and Miss Minnie Bannister join forces to create a special laundry soup for relief of the dirty. The special ingredient places the entire cast in a fowl play.

'...the ex-regimental strangler's ragged underpants were devine'
WESTERN MALE

The main characters

Music Hall artistes	Peter Sellers
	Kenneth Connor
House Manager	Peter Sellers
Lew	Peter Sellers
Moriarty	Spike Milligan
Grytpype-Thynne	Peter Sellers
Bank Teller	Peter Sellers
Bank Manager 'Jim'	Spike Milligan
Eccles	Spike Milligan
Nurse	Peter Sellers
Governor Wolfit	Spike Milligan
Bluebottle	Peter Sellers
Major Denis Bloodnok	Peter Sellers
Minnie Bannister	Spike Milligan
Henry Crun	Peter Sellers
Old Uncle Oscar	Kenneth Connor

(Harry Secombe was indisposed for this broadcast)

The Ray Ellington Quartet
Max Geldray
Orchestra conducted by Wally Stott
Announcer: Wallace Greenslade
Script by Spike Milligan
Produced by John Browell

THE £50 CURE

BILL   This is the BBC Home Service, away with dull care, let the joy bells ring, Huzzah!

GRAMS   **DEAD MARCH FROM 'HAMLET': SOLEMN TREAD OF FUNERAL CORTEGE WAILS OF PROFESSIONAL JEWISH MOURNERS IN THE BACKGROUND — ECCLES SINGING**

KEN   By Jove, it's a merry singing funeral. Don't take it so hard folks, it's only a trial one for Eccles. And now for an encore I'll sing a little song entitled 'Looking through the knot-hole in Grandma's wooden leg'. Maestro please . . . . thank you (*sings*), 'Long long ago in the wilds of Australia . . . .

PETER   I say, I say, You look a sporting gentleman to me, You look like a sporting man.

KEN   How dare you interrupt my act with 'I say, I says' while I'm trying to entertain these nice nutty ladies and gentlemen here.

PETER   Tell me, I say . . . . tell me I say, if it takes a chicken ten days to eat forty pounds of sawdust how long would it take to lay a ten-ton wooden egg . . . .? Do you give up?

KEN   Yes.

PETER   You do . . . .? So did the chicken!

KEN   I say, now look here, look here . . . .

PETER   Tell me, tell me, tell me Mister Man, tell me Mister man can a woman with a wooden leg change a pound note?

KEN   Can a woman with a wooden leg change a pound note? Of course she can!

PETER   No she can't, you see she's only got 'Half a Nicker' ha ha!

KEN   Would you kindly leave the green-gate. It doesn't really matter 'cos we're still good friends . . . . you see becauseeeee!

ORCHESTRA   **THREE NOTE INTRO INTO 'ARM IN ARM TOGETHER' — LAST EIGHT BARS**

PETER & KEN	(*sing*) Arm in Arm together just like we used to be arm in arm through destinyyyyyyyyyy.
ORCHESTRA	**TATTY 'I WANT TO BE HAPPY' PLAY OFF. SEGUE INTO 'MOONLIGHT MADONNA' VIOLIN, CLARINET, TROMBONE LEAD ON FLOOR. ALL PLAYING MELODY.**
HOUSE MANAGER	(*over mikes*) And now, if you'll pardon the expression, number two on your programme is the world famous Continental act Le Trois Toms des Acton.
BILL	(*seat in the circle voice*) And onto the stage come three tatty men wearing wigs, leotards and partial boots, the anchor man has a hearing aid on his shin.
KEN	Hoi . . . . huo hup!
ORCHESTRA	**ROLL ON DRUMS. CYMBAL CRASH.**
GRAMS	**TATTY APPLAUSE. DISTANT RASPBERRY.**
KEN	And now we take pleasure in performing the death-defying Great Pyramid . . . Hoi! Hup!
ORCHESTRA	**SLOW BUILDING ROLL ON DRUMS**
TRIO	DREADFUL STRAINS. F.X. ODD CLICKS AND CLACKS. OLD BONES CREAKING.
HOUSE MANAGER	(*over above*) And the Trois Toms des Acton strain to make a sub-human pyramid of knees.
GRAMS	**SOUND OF PLANK ON THE STAGE STARTING TO BREAK — FINALLY THE WHOLE TRIO CRASH THROUGH THE WOODEN STAGE — TRIO SCREAM**
HOUSE MANAGER	Oh dear, they've all gone through the stage, they'll be killed!
ORCHESTRA	**'I WANT TO BE HAPPY' — LAST 8 BARS**
KEN	Ohh my leg, it's gone below the waist.
LEW	(*approach*) What's happened? Why aren't you on the stage then?
KEN	I've broken my right leg.
LEW	Only one? Get back on that stage do you hear!
KEN	I refuse!
MAX	You'd better do as he says boy, or we'll never work again.
KEN	Righttttt come here, come here. Help me up with your conk.
F.X.	**CRACK OR SNAP OF LEG-BONE BREAKING**
KEN	Oh, there goes the other one!
LEW	Two broken legs! Give me the mike. Hello ladies and gentlemen, presenting Neddie Seagoon in his impression of Toulouse Lautrec!
F.X.	**BICYCLE BELL**
MORIARTY	STOP! Ferme Hoi La.

GRYTPYPE-THYNNE	I second Ferme Hoi La.
KEN	In our midst if not sooner, rode two men wearing nude clothes. On a unicycle they were. Their bodies driven by legs and their legs driven by feet.
GRYTPYPE-THYNNE	Nothing but the best for us, Kennie. My card de Jour.
KEN	(*reads*) 'Doctors Moriarty and Thynne, surgeons, tree fellers and old women hit while you wait.'
MORIARTY	We must examine this wreck . . . . say ahhhhh.
KEN	Ahhhhhhhhhhhhhhh . . . .
MORIARTY	Come little hairy Kennie let us give you a free diagnosis . . . . now put your head on that anvil.
F.X.	**SLAM OF SHOVEL ON ANVIL — KEN SCREAMS**
MORIARTY	Just as I thought! A fractured skull!
GRYTPYPE-THYNNE	Yes, Ken, now let us examine your wallet.
F.X.	**BOLTS, CHAINS, LOCKS, KEYS**
GRAMS	**TAPPING ON HUGE EMPTY WATER TANK WITH A SMALL MALLET. (TO GIVE THAT HOLLOW SOUND)**
GRYTPYPE-THYNNE	Empty, by Jupiter . . . . Kennie you're suffering from advanced poverty.
KEN	I say, is that dangerous?
GRYTPYPE-THYNNE	If not checked it can lead to bankruptcy, and the Pauper's Krutt, the dreaded disease that took poor Max Geldray's conk away in its prime.
MAX	Yes, I got it bad and dat ain't good, boy.
KEN	You going to play mate?
MAX	Yes, dat means that you're going back for —
OMNES	**The Brandyyyyyy**
GRAMS	**THUNDERING OF DEPARTING BOOTS**

MAX & ORCHESTRA	**MUSIC**
	(applause)
MAX	Thank you ladies and gentlemen.
BILL	During Mr Geldray's conk, the great surgeons worked on Connor's poverty.
F.X.	**WRITING**
MORIARTY	Now little hairy Kennie, here is a National Health Prescription on hair.
KEN	I see. *(reads)* '£50 to be taken once a week until better'. . . . money? Ha, ha, ha . . . . so that's the cure for poverty.
GRYTPYPE-THYNNE	Yes . . . . it took a lot of Lab work but we found it.
KEN	Well, I'll get round to the bank and have this made-up.
MORIARTY	Not with those naughty broken legs Kennie . . . . we'll keep them until they're mended . . . . now let us rest your body on this pair of skates and awayyyyyyyyyyy . . . . goodbye!
GRAMS	**KEN SINGING: AND THE SOUND OF A PAIR OF SKATES DEPARTING DOWN A PAVED-PAVEMENT**
GRYTPYPE-THYNNE	Now Moriarty, our master-plan, put on this mask, strap it to your knee, then glue this bearded wig to your teeth.
MORIARTY	There, how do I look?
GRYTPYPE-THYNNE	It's too early to say.
MORIARTY	Look out, here comes an announcement . . . .
BILL	And now by arrangement with America . . . . the sound of the Bank of England.
F.X.	**PENNY DROPPED ON TO SOMETHING RESONANT**
BANK TELLER	We had a beastly day, dear.
KEN	Hello Merry bank teller.
BANK TELLER	I say, what's this? A sack of potatoes on skates?
KEN	It's only a temporary measure, now call your manager.
BANK MANAGER	What is it Jim what is Jimmmmmmmmm.
KEN	Make up this prescription Jimmmmmmmmmm.
BANK MANAGER	£50 on the National Health . . . . that will cost you a shilling Jimmmmmmmmmmmm.
KEN	Touche. Jimmmmmm . . . .
BANK MANAGER	Miss Lum, make up a bottle of £50.
F.X.	**SCOOP OF MONEY (COINS)**
BANK MANAGER	There Jim. There Jimmmmm . . . .

KEN	Thank you, thank you my man, and here's a tip.
BANK MANAGER	A tip? A piece of cork?
KEN	Yes, it's a cork tip!
ORCHESTRA	**TA RA CHORD**
GRAMS	**OVATION, SCREAMS AND CHEERS**
KEN	Stop . . . . it wasn't that funny folks . . . . it wasn't that funny.
GRYTPYPE-THYNNE	Huhhhhh.
F.X.	**THUD. (NOT TEMPLE BLOCK) THUD**
KEN	Ohh, nutted by men with masked knees . . . Ohh . . .
MORIARTY	Got him! Now get this bottle of money, and off we go . . . .
GRAMS	**WHOOSH**
WILLIUM	(*blows hot break on police whistle*) 'Ello sir 'ello, I was reading the Police Gazette and I saw your Advert that read 'help, I have been attacked, apply to the supine body on the pavement'.

145

KEN	Yes, I've just had my medicine stolen.
WILLIUM	Stolen on it yern?
KEN	Yern.
WILLIUM	Arnn! Now, where's me mate's note-book, ah here it is on top of the Eiffel Tower. Now den . . . . What was this medicine called?
KEN	It's called £50.
ECCLES	Hello Ken!
KEN	Hello Eccles.
ECCLES	Well I better be gettin' along.
WILLIUM	'Ere, 'ere wait a minute aren't you the Minister who built that highway that fell to bits?
ECCLES	No.
WILLIUM	Ohh, well it was somebody like you, I know.

ECCLES	I arrest you for the murder of Bluebottle.
WILLIUM	He ain't dead!
ECCLES	Oh well, you watch it, that's all.
MORIARTY	Look Grytpype, it's poor Kennie . . . . and his wallet is still empty.
F.X.	**FURIOUS WRITING**
GRYTPYPE-THYNNE	There Ken, a fresh prescription for £50 . . . . now let's get him to a hospital.
GRAMS	**PAIR OF SKATES ON PAVEMENT**
KEN	Oh, thank heaven you came Doctor, some swine's robbed my £50 of medicine and . . . . *(speed up)*
BILL	Now, a National Health Hospital.
GRAMS	**PALM COURT TRIO: TEA CUPS IN DISTANCE**
NURSE	Time for your naughty medicine Mr Connor.

KEN	Oh Nurse .... ha ha I didn't see you ....
NURSE	You are naughty .... say Ahhhhhhhh!
F.X.	**MONEY BEING SCOOPED DOWN HIS THROAT**
KEN	(*mouthing*) Ahh £50 ... my poverty feels better already ... gad, I feel fit.
ECCLES	Hello dear .... well, how's the patient?
NURSE	Ohh hello handsome.
ECCLES	Ohh, you're a good looking fella too.
KEN	Silly Eccles, this nurse is a woman.
ECCLES	Oh well, he's a good-lookin' woman, isn't he ....
NURSE	Are you married?
ECCLES	Yer.
NURSE	Your poor wife.
ECCLES	Yer. But the girl next door, ohhh ho ho ho ho ....
KEN	He's growing up folks, it had to come.
ECCLES	Hello folks, hello folks and now folks here's my latest record folks.
GRAMS	**VERY OLD HILTON RECORD: RECORD ECCLES SINGING OVER THE TOP OF IT**
F.X.	**PISTOL SHOT**
ECCLES	Ohhhhh ....
KEN	Bad news folks devine, while that record was in the oven, I was dragged from my sick bed, and thrown in Holloway Women's Prison. Oh tragedy, incarcerated in a women's prison, I have a request for liberty, give me twenty-four hours.
GOVERNOR WOLFIT	Right, hold out your steaming hat.
F.X.	**PILE OF RUBBISH**
GOVERNOR WOLFIT	There, and it's all in minutes.
KEN	Ta sir, in the time given I will try to trace the villains and regain possession of my legs.
GOVERNOR WOLFIT	Right Warden, let him go, but keep him on a chain.
RAY	Right, I'll pay it out. Off you go mate.
GRAMS	**PAIR OF SKATES FREE WHEELING START SLOW AND GET FAST. CHAIN PAYING OUT. KEN SINGS: 'China, my Island homeland of the free .... I've got the etc. etc.'**
BILL	And as the body of Connor skates into the night we find a lone-vinegar sipper called Ray Ellington who sings devine.

RAY ELLINGTON QUARTET	**MUSIC**

(*applause*)

BILL	Could I have some music with this announcement please.
BLUEBOTTLE	All right den Wal, I been waitin' for dis bit (*sings*) 'Does the Christmas Puddin' lose its flavour up the chimney overnight.' (*sings behind*)
BILL	Ta. Poor Connor is travelling on a roller skate, his legs being filched by the two fiend doctors. We find him on a lonely Sussex moor, a chain round his neck, the other end attached to Holloway Prison.
GRAMS	**HOWLING WIND AND RAIN. ROLLER SKATES APPROACH CHAIN PAYING OUT.**
KEN	Ohhh what a night folks. Ten miles I have travelled and no signs of the two doctors. I must complain to the AA, the BB and the CC, or in English yes yes.
BLUEBOTTLE	Can I stop singing now, Captain? My nose has started to bleed.

149

KEN	Go away lad will you, I'm acting.
BLUEBOTTLE	Oh, could I act wid you den?
KEN	Yes, but keep quiet.
BLUEBOTTLE	Can I be your stand in?
KEN	Alright. Stand in that hole over there.
BLUEBOTTLE	Cor standing in a hole! I wish my mum could see me now . . . . Hello, Mum, Dad, Rene, Eileen and Dave, I am quite well and acting on radio keep the dinner in the oven, 'cos I won't be . . . .
F.X.	**SLAPSTICK**
BLUEBOTTLE	Oh you swine, you've hurt my shirt.
KEN	Shut up child. I'll lay me down on this tatty piece of ground called England. (*sleeps*)
BLUEBOTTLE	(*goes off*) I'm goin' home . . . . I don't want to stay and play . . . . (*I'm going threats*) Do you hear me? I'm goin' . . . .
GRAMS	**SOUND OF GREAT THUNDERING SOLO OF 'OLD COMRADES' OVER SUDDENLY. HAVE AN EXPLOSION. RAIN ON TIN ROOF. SKITTLES IN BOWLING ALLEY. EXPLOSION. SERIES OF FIREWORKS. (THE CRACKERS THAT GO OFF RAPIDLY ONE AFTER OTHER) ONE OR TWO THUNDER FLASHES. SUPERIMPOSED OVER SOLO OF 'OLD COMRADES'**
BLOODNOK	(*screams and hollers over the above*) Ohhh, dear dearrrrrrr, that wasn't in the music.
KEN	You, you sir, how dare you break into my private sleep.
BLOODNOK	Well, I saw your mouth open so I came in.
KEN	Well get out of my mouth and Mind the Jaws!
GRAMS	**TUBE TRAIN DOORS CLOSE**
BLOODNOK	Ohh, just in time. Wait a moment Sir. Lift-up your trouser leg.
F.X.	**WOODEN VENETIAN BLIND GOES UP**
BLOODNOK	Ohh, just as I thought, the ragged-underpants of gunner Connor, ex-regimental strangler.
KEN	Exposed! Tell me, how do you know my terrible secret?
BLOODNOK	The war lad, France and the Low Countries. Remember?
KEN	Err . . . .
BLOODNOK	The invasion, Salerno. Remember we spent that night in a field together?
KEN	Sheila Francis, 601 ATS Company. Darling, what hit you?
BLOODNOK	Put me down you blind military fool! I'm not her do you hear me. I'm . . . . and I quote from this dishonourable discharge paper . . . . I'm . . . . no, better still, I'll unveil myself.

F.X.	**RIPPING OF CANVAS**
KEN	Great Heavens! Major Denis Bloodnok, coward and bar, what are you doing on a lonely Sussex moor?
BLOODNOK	The old trouble lad, you know. You never know where you find them. You see I'm on a world tuba playing tour of England.
KEN	It must be hell in there.
BLOODNOK	It is. Look we can't stand here in this rain on a lonely moor, people will think we're avoiding them. Wait a minute, give me a rock, there's something behind that tree. Huhh . . . .
GRAMS	**DISTANT SOUND OF STONE HITTING BLUEBOTTLES HEAD. BLUEBOTTLE Oeeeeeee. Ohhhhhh . . . swine man Bloodnok, you've krinned my Plitts. (SPEED UP AS BLUEBOTTLE SPEAKS)**
ORCHESTRA	**MAD LINK. SUDDEN RUSH OF COMPLICATED 5/4 MUSIC. PAUSE. ANOTHER MAD RUSH TO PLAY THE PHRASE . . . ALL THE ORCHESTRA GIVE A LOUD YELL . . . . GEORGE CHISHOLM SINGS 'OOOOOOOOOO' ORCHESTRA PLAY THE PHRASE AFTER HIM (BUSK IT) . . . . TROMBONE SOLO.**
GRAMS	**GREAT EXPLOSION**
ORCHESTRA	**BURSTS INTO MAD RUSH OF GRAND FINALE GETS FASTER AND FASTER**
GRAMS	**SCREECH OF BRAKES, CAR CRASHES INTO PLATE-GLASS SHOP-WINDOW. THREE OR FOUR CUCKOOS FROM GENUINE CUCKOOS.**

MORIARTY	And there's more where that came from.
F.X.	**SLAPSTICK**
MORIARTY	Owwwwwwwwwwwww . . . .
BILL	For no reason other than a paucity of creative continuity, we go to an outlandish old Victorian manor. If you roll up your trousers you will hear it quite clearly.
GRAMS	**BOILING CAULDRON**
MINNIE	Ha ha ha ha he he he, boil cauldron boil, eye of newt, leg of toad, eagles knee, shell of snail, he he he he, ha ha ha ha.
CRUN	Ah mistress Bannister, what is that hellish fiend brew?
MINNIE	It's your laundry Henery, I'm making a laundry soup.
F.X.	**DOOR OPENS**
MINNIE	Make way for him Henery, stand back!
OLD UNCLE OSCAR	Morninggggggggggg ahhh Min ahhhhhhh . . . .
MINNIE	He's saying good morning Henery. Morning morning Uncle Oscar!
CRUN	He's a bit mutton. What did you do with his ear trumpet? Uncle, what are you doing out of your grave so early?
OLD UNCLE OSCAR	I'm feeling better. Hot porridge, ahhhhh.
CRUN	He wants hot porridge, Min.
MINNIE	Sip this nice steaming laundry soup.
OLD UNCLE OSCAR	Mamam ahhhhahahah sipppppppp ahhhhhhh . . . .
MINNIE	Drink it all down.
GRAMS	**THUD AND STARTLED CHICKEN CLUCKS — CONTINUES INTERMITTENTLY**

CRUN	Ohhh Min, it's turned him into a male chicken!
MINNIE	Oh dear, Oh dear, well give him an aspirin and put him to bed.
CRUN	Yes, perhaps it will wear off by morning, if not (*glee*) chicken for Sunday dinner Min .... ha he he ....
F.X.	**STONE THROUGH GLASS WINDOW LANDS ON FLOOR**
MINNIE	Lawks, a stone through the window.
CRUN	There's something attached to it.
KEN	It's me folks, Kennie. And this is my way of saying have you got lodgings?
CRUN	Yes, I've got 'em very bad.
MINNIE	Look you could share the steam attic with two gentlemen doctors upstairs.
KEN	Two gentlemen doctors? Send for the police, those men are criminals.
ORCHESTRA	**DRAMATIC MUSIC**
GRAMS	**SOUNDS OF WAILING POLICE SIRENS**
MORIARTY	Ahh what's that? Ahhhhhh Police, they've surrounded the house, we're surrounded.
GRYTPYPE-THYNNE	What? Somebody's tipped them off. Get the Gatling gun loaded and put this string in your shoulder holster.
GRAMS	**WILLIUM (OFF) You in there, gie yer self up on it, you're surrounded, come out with your hands up or we'll say rude words on you.**
KEN	Throw my legs out you naughty men!
GRYTPYPE-THYNNE	One step nearer Kennie, and your legs will go in the mincer.

153

KEN	You wouldn't dare mince the legs of a gooner.
GRYTPYPE-THYNNE	No? I tell you we're desperate men.
KEN	You must be, to be on a show like this.
GRYTPYPE-THYNNE	You're ad-libbing.
KEN	I'm not ad-libbing at all. Bluebottle, take this conker and get my legs back.
BLUEBOTTLE	O.K. Captain, I have got my Finchley gang with me . . . ready men?
GRAMS	**A DOZEN BLUEBOTTLES ALL YELL 'YESSSSSSSS'**
BLUEBOTTLE	Charge eeeeeeeeeceeeeeeeee.
GRAMS	**YELLS OF ALL THE BLUEBOTTLES ALL SHOUTING 'RAY FOR BOTTLE' ETC. AND DEPARTING LITTLE BOOTS**
KEN	There they go little heroes all. All that night folks the battle for my legs it raged.
GRAMS	**BLUEBOTTLES ALL SHOUTING 'BANG BANG BANG, YOU'RE DEAD'**
F.X.	**DOOR OPENS**
MORIARTY	Stop! We give up. Those pimples and elastic string, they overpower us. Come in little boys, and have some of this nice laundry food.
GRAMS	**GREAT RUSH OF BOOTS AS THEY RUSH IN**
GRYTPYPE-THYNNE	Come in, let's all sip some of this special 'Minnie Bannister' soup.
KEN	I can see what's coming . . . . but here goes.
OMNES	**SIPPING**
GRAMS	**SIPPING SOUNDS . . . . GRADUALLY CHICKENS START TO CLUCK. CLUCKING . . . . EVERYWHERE CHICKENS CLUCKING**
OMNES	**WITH THE ABOVE. ALL CLUCK.**
CRUN	Min, what did you put in the laundry soup?
BILL	Ladies and Gentlemen, with the entire cast unfortunately turned into brood chickens, we are forced to close this series of Goon Shows. The entire audience will now join hands, teeth and knees with the orchestra and sing.
PIANO	**CHORD INTO: 'WE'LL GATHER LILACS'**
CAST & ORCHESTRA	**(SINGS) WE'LL GATHER LILACS** *(see accompanying words)*
GRAMS	**OVER THE ABOVE SINGING. CHICKENS KEEP CLUCKING IN A STARTLED MANNER**
ORCHESTRA	**'OLD COMRADES' PLAY OUT**

WE'LL GATHER LILACS

We'll gather-er li-lacs in the spring a-gain,

And walk to-geth-er down an Eng-lish lane,

Un-til our hearts have learned to sing a-gain,

When you come home once more.

And in the eve-'ning by the fire-light's glow

Your'll hold me close and nev-er let me go

Your eyes will tell me all I want to know

When you come home once more.

BACKWORD
HARRY SECOMBE

It is a never-ending source of amazement to the three of us that even today, twelve years after the last regular Goon series, we are still referred to in the Press as 'ex-Goon' or 'Arch-Goon'. At the time of writing 'The Ying Tong Song', which was recorded about seventeen years ago, has reached the 'charts'.

It seems that old Goons, like old soldiers, never die and show little signs of fading away, though in my case that would not be such a bad idea. There is a quality of indestructibility in Spike's creations which seems to defy the normal processes of Nature. If ever, or *whenever* the Big Bang comes I have the feeling that the dreadful silence which follows it will be broken by a dishevelled Eccles rising Phoenix-like from the ashes saying 'How about dat?'. He will be joined by a shattered Bluebottle saying 'I don't like this game'. And as they disappear hand-in-hand over the horizon there will be cries of 'Wait for me' as Bloodnok, Grytpype, Neddie and company emerge from their hiding places to go bounding away after them.

They might then create a lunatic new world which could be infinitely preferable to the old one. Eccles for King, folks.

AUGUST 1973

$\frac{6}{10}$

S. Milligan.
See me after class